Beginners' Arabic

Frances Altorfer and
Mairi Smart

First published in Great Britain as *Get Started in Arabic* by Hodder & Stoughton in 2013

This edition published by Teach Yourself in 2024

An imprint of John Murray Press

1

Illustrations by Frances Altorfer and Nadene Naude (Beehive Illustration)

Editorial support from Haremi Ltd and Frances Amrani

A CIP catalogue record for this title is available from the British Library

Paperback ISBN 9781399818261

ebook ISBN 9781399818438

Typeset by Integra Software Services Pvt. Ltd., Pondicherry, India

Printed and bound in Great Britain by Clays Ltd, Elcograf S.p.A.

John Murray Press policy is to use papers that are natural, renewable and recyclable products and made from wood grown in sustainable forests. The logging and manufacturing processes are expected to conform to the environmental regulations of the country of origin.

John Murray Press	Nicholas Brealey Publishing
Carmelite House	Hachette Book Group
50 Victoria Embankment	Market Place, Center 53, State Street
London EC4Y 0DZ	Boston, MA 02109, USA

www.teachyourself.com

John Murray Press, part of Hodder & Stoughton Limited

An Hachette UK company

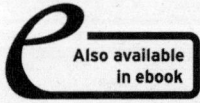
Also available in ebook

Contents

About the authors   **v**

Introduction to the Arabic language   **vi**

How to use this book   **viii**

Learn to learn!   **xi**

The Arabic script   **xv**

Pronunciation   **xix**

1   **áhlan wa sáhlan!** *Hello!*   **2**
Say *hello* and *goodbye* • Use common greetings
• Introduce yourself and others • Say where you're from
• Ask someone where they are from

2   **ta-takállam :árabi?** *Do you speak Arabic?*   **16**
State your nationality • Say what languages you speak
• Recognize and use numbers 0–10 • Ask for and
give phone numbers • Ask for someone on the phone

3   **al-:áa'ilah** *The family*   **30**
Say where you live • Talk about people's occupations
• Talk about your family • Talk about more than
one person

Review: Units 1–3   **42**

4   **kam as-sáa:ah?** *What time is it?*   **46**
Ask for and tell the time • Ask when places are open or
closed • Talk about days of the week • Talk about different
times of day

5   **bi-kám háadha?** *How much is this?*   **58**
Ask for an item in a shop • Recognize prices online
• Ask for something different • Say what colour
something is • Recognize and use numbers 11 to 1 million
• Ask about prices

6   **aish ti-ríid tíshrab?** *What would you like to drink?*   **72**
         Say what you like to eat and drink • Say what you like and
         dislike • Say what you prefer • Order snacks and drinks

         Review: Units 4–6   **84**

7   **fi l-madíinah** *In the city*   **90**
         Ask for places in a town • Ask where places are • Ask for
         and give directions • Direct a taxi driver to your
         destination

8   **li-wain?** *Where to?*   **102**
         Book and buy travel tickets • Hire a car • Buy petrol
         and deal with simple car problems

9   **aish tiHíbb tisáwwi?** *What do you like to do?*   **114**
         Talk about what you do in your free time • Say what you
         will do and when • Say how often you do things
         • Make arrangements to meet people

10   **li-wain ruHt fi l-ijáazah?** *Where did you go on holiday?*   **128**
         Say the months of the year • Talk about your last holiday
         • Say what you have done • Describe the weather

         Review: Units 7–10   **142**

         Answer key   **148**

         Core vocabulary   **170**

         Useful phrases   **176**

         List of verbs   **177**

         Acknowledgements   **178**

         Photo credits   **179**

         Can-do statements   **180**

About the authors

Both authors are linguists of long experience and are familiar with the Arab countries, their society, religion and culture.

Frances Altorfer was born in England to a Swiss father and an English mother. She grew up in Kenya, where she developed her interest in languages by learning French, German and Russian at school and Swahili at home. Fran has lived in the Middle East, and travels regularly to the Gulf countries. She has many years of experience as a language teacher, using the most up-to-date teaching methods. She is co-author of several Arabic language books, including *Complete Arabic* (Teach Yourself, 2016) and *Complete Spoken Arabic* (Teach Yourself, 2016).

Mairi Smart was born in Cambridge to a family of linguists. Her father ignited her interest in Arabic, which she studied with German at university. She has lived in Egypt, Switzerland, Japan and the Gulf. A passionate linguist and teacher with almost 20 years' experience, Mairi has taught Arabic, German, French, Japanese and English to students of wide-ranging ages and abilities, using the latest interactive teaching methods. She taught Arabic for many years in the Middle East.

Frances and Mairi firmly believe that it's never too late for you to learn a new language, and that speaking even a small amount helps you to connect with people from other countries on a more personal level. Both Frances and Mairi encourage you to do this by making explanations within *Beginners' Arabic* as clear as possible, and by finding ways to make learning Arabic engaging and fun.

Introduction to the Arabic language

There are three main types of Arabic: **Classical Arabic**, **Modern Standard Arabic** and **Colloquial Arabic**.

The first, **Classical Arabic**, is the Arabic of the Holy Koran, or Qur'an. It is read and recited by millions of Muslims, many of whom do not speak Arabic as a first language, all over the world, and has hardly changed since the first dictionary was written in the 8th century AD. This is quite amazing, considering that it would be impossible for the average person to read 8th-century English nowadays. Classical Arabic is only used in the Qur'an and early poetry.

The second type is the modern written language, **Modern Standard Arabic** (MSA), and is hardly ever used in speech, except in formal situations such as news broadcasts or political speeches. Many Arabic speakers believe that written Arabic is the only 'pure' Arabic, but no one speaks it and, in fact, even academics find it hard to keep speaking MSA for very long. So if you want to speak and understand Arabic, instead of only reading and writing it, you need to learn the third type, **Colloquial Arabic**, and this is the purpose of *Beginners' Arabic*.

The **Colloquial Arabic** spoken in daily life by nearly 300 million people is not just one language, but a series of dialects, varying widely from country to country, just as the English spoken in Scotland is different to the English spoken in Australia or Kentucky, USA. These dialects fall into four or five main groups, and in this book you will learn the spoken Arabic of one of the larger groups, Gulf Arabic.

Gulf Arabic is spoken in the Arabian Peninsula and Iraq. Even within the Gulf region, there are differences from one country to another, but people still easily understand each other. For instance, in some regions, the word for *they go* is **yiruuHúun**, and in other parts the word used is **yirúuHuu**, without the final **-n**, but you will be understood whichever form you use. After you have worked through this book, you will have a good grounding in the basic features of Arabic and you will be able to adapt easily to the dialects of most other Arabic-speaking countries.

Colloquial Arabic is not often written down, except in cartoons and TV drama scripts or text messages between friends. In *Beginners' Arabic* we will show you how to read the MSA script so that you can understand common everyday signs and notices. Many people are put off by the apparently difficult script. In fact, this is one of the most rewarding aspects of learning Arabic, and once you have mastered all 28 letters, it is easy to read and write. Arabic is a highly phonetic language, i.e. it is written as it sounds, and has very few of the spelling oddities of English such as *write/right* or *cough/through*.

It is worth mentioning the influence of Islam on the Arabic language since this will be evident to you right from the start. Indeed, it is because of Islam that Arabic acquired the universal status which it has continued to enjoy since the Middle Ages, when it emerged as a world language. A rich and expressive language, Arabic plays an important part in preserving the culture of the Arabic-speaking people. The religious phrases and expressions that are introduced in this book are very widely heard, and can be used freely by Muslims and non-Muslims alike.

People from Arabic-speaking countries very much appreciate any attempt to learn their language, and your every effort will be greeted with amazement and enthusiasm. Knowledge of Arabic is the key to a society of very friendly people, which is often thought difficult to penetrate. Being able to speak even a little Arabic will enhance your social life, and, in the worlds of business or tourism, can open doors that would otherwise remain firmly closed.

We wish you every success as you embark on your Arabic journey and hope you will come to love the language, its people and their culture as much as we do.

How to use this book

A little goes a long way!

Try to use the book little and often, rather than for long stretches at a time (between 15 and 30 minutes if possible, rather than two to three hours in one session). This will help you to create a study habit, much in the same way you would a sport or music. Leave the book somewhere handy so that you can pick it up for just a few minutes to refresh your memory again with what you were looking at the time before.

Before you start, make a plan!

Setting goals affects the programming of your brain, strengthening neural pathways and ultimately making it more likely that you will achieve those goals. Before you begin, think about how much time you want to devote to learning, which skills or areas you want to focus on, and identify specific ideas you want to be able to communicate or activities you want to engage in.

Track your progress!

Start a notebook to use for study, where you can create vocabulary lists, a grammar summary, questions you'd like answered, etc. Keep track of your resources--write down the names of movies, podcasts, songs or blogs you like, and jot down a few words or expressions you may have recognized or learned. The more you can reflect on your learning process, the deeper your connection with the language will be. If you need more guidance in this process, we recommend the Teach Yourself *Fluentish: Language Learning Planner & Journal* by Jo Franco.

Use the tools at the beginning of each unit to help you set goals, plan your time, and keep track of the work you do.

IN THIS UNIT, YOU WILL LEARN HOW TO

Each unit begins with an overview of the language you will be learning and skills you will be acquiring.

MY PROGRESS TRACKER

Use the progress tracker to plan your study time and to keep a record of what you've accomplished. The first column tracks time, and the remaining 4 columns represent the skills you'll be working on: listening, pronunciation, reading and spoken interaction.

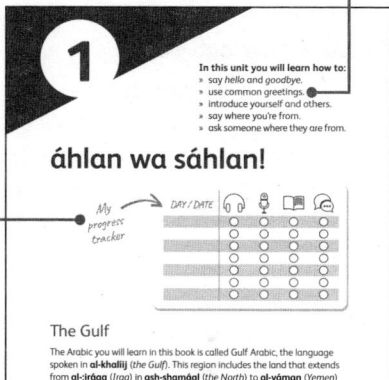

Personalize the tracker: Instead of the date or day, you can enter an increment of time (15 minutes, 1 hour...). Add columns for culture, vocabulary, grammar or any other area you wish to focus on. Give yourself a star when you feel you've done particularly well. Make it your own! Review your tracker regularly and see which areas could use more practice.

Use the **Self check** at the end of each unit to evaluate your progress.

Try to practice each skill every day.

The icons in the progress tracker are used throughout the book to help you easily identify and locate the skills you want to practice:

     Listening skills

     Speaking – pronunciation skills

     Reading skills

     Speaking – conversation skills

Remember: there are many ways to build your skills in addition to those provided in this book: use a language-learning app, listen to music or podcasts, watch TV shows or movies, go to a restaurant, follow Arabic social media accounts, read blogs, newspapers or magazines, switch the language settings in your apps to Arabic, or sign up for a language exchange or a tutor.

Learn to learn!

The Discovery method

There are lots of philosophies and approaches to language learning, some practical, some quite unconventional, and far too many to list here. Perhaps you know of a few, or even have some techniques of your own. In this book we have incorporated the **Discovery method** of learning, a sort of DIY approach to language learning. What this means is that you will be encouraged throughout the course to engage your mind and figure out the language for yourself, through identifying patterns, understanding grammar concepts, noticing words that are similar to English or similar to ones you have seen in earlier units, and more.

Simply put, if you figure something out for yourself, you're more likely to understand it. And when you use what you've learned, you're more likely to remember it. And because many of the essential but (let's admit it!) daunting details, such as grammar rules, are introduced through the Discovery method, you'll have more fun while learning. Soon, the language will start to make sense and you'll be relying on your own intuition to construct original sentences independently, not just listening and repeating.

Everyone can succeed in learning a language – the key is to know how to learn it.

How to be a successful language learner

There are many strategies that can help you become a successful language learner. Different people have different learning styles and some of these approaches will be more effective for you than others. Use this list as a point of inspiration when you want to find the most effective ways to advance your skills and begin your journey to fluency.

Make a habit out of learning.

Vocabulary

Words are the building blocks of language. The more you use the words you're introduced to, the more quickly they'll lodge into your memory. These study tips will help you remember better:

▶ Say the words out loud as you read them. Listen to the audio several times.

▶ Write the words over and over again. Create flash cards, drawings and mind maps.

▶ It helps to group new words in categories, like food or furniture, or according to the situations in which they occur, e.g. restaurant, hotel, sight-seeing, or their functions, e.g. greetings, thanks, apologizing.

▶ Cover up the English side of the vocabulary list and see if you remember the meaning of the word. Then cover up the Arabic side, and see if you can remember the word itself.

▶ Write words for objects around your house and stick them to objects.

Grammar

Grammar gives your language structure. It allows you to experiment with the vocabulary you learn because you'll understand how they work together to create meaning. In other words, you'll begin to develop a feel for the language. Here are some tips to help you study more effectively:

▶ Write your own grammar glossary and add new information and examples as you go.

▶ Experiment with grammar rules. Use old vocabulary to practice new grammar structures.

▶ Try to find examples of grammar in conversations or other articles.

▶ When you learn a new verb form, review other verbs you know that follow the same pattern.

▶ Compare Arabic structures with your own language or other languages you may already speak. Try to find out some rules on your own and be ready to spot the exceptions.

 # Pronunciation

The best way to improve your pronunciation is simply to practice as much as possible Study individual sounds first, then full words and sentences. Don't forget, it's not just about pronouncing letters and words correctly, but using the right intonation. So, when practicing words and sentences, mimic the rising and falling intonation of native speakers.

▶ Repeat all of the conversations, line by line. Listen to yourself and try to mimic what you hear.
▶ Record yourself and compare yourself to the recordings.
▶ Make a list of words that give you trouble and practice them.

Listening and reading

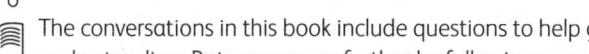 The conversations in this book include questions to help guide you in your understanding. But you can go further by following some of these tips.

▶ Imagine the situation. Try to imagine where the scene is taking place and who the main characters are. Let your experience of the world help you guess the meaning of the conversation, e.g. if a conversation takes place in a café, you can predict the kind of vocabulary that will be used.
▶ Concentrate on the main part. When watching a foreign movie you usually get the meaning of the whole story from a few individual shots. Understanding a foreign conversation or article is similar. Concentrate on the main message and don't worry about individual words.
▶ Familiarize yourself with the words and Arabic script introduced in the Reading Arabic sections in each unit.

Speaking

The greatest obstacle to speaking a new language is the fear of making a mistake. Keep in mind that you make mistakes in your own language-- it's simply part of the human condition. Accept it. Focus on the message. Most errors are not serious and they will not affect the meaning, so concentrate on getting your message across and use the mistakes as learning opportunities.

Here are some useful tips to help you practice speaking Arabic:

▶ When you're going about your day, e.g. buying groceries, ordering food and drinks, do it in Arabic in your mind! Look at objects around you and try to name them in Arabic. Look at people around you and try to describe them in detail.

▶ Answer all of the questions in the book out loud. Say the dialogues out loud, then try to replace sentences with ones that are true for you. Role-play different situations in the book.

▶ Keep talking. The best way to improve your fluency in a language is to talk every time you have the opportunity to do so: keep the conversations flowing and don't worry about the mistakes. If you get stuck for a particular word, don't let the conversation stop; simplify what you want to say; paraphrase or replace the unknown word with one you do know.

Learning a language takes work. But the work can be a lot of fun! So, let's begin!

The Arabic script

The Arabic script looks difficult because it is so different from what we are used to. In fact, the Arabic script is easy to master and with practice you will soon be able to distinguish the letters, as Arabic is generally written exactly as it sounds.

General facts about the Arabic script

▶ The basic Arabic alphabet has 28 letters.
▶ Arabic is written (and read!) from right to left – in the opposite direction to English.
▶ Like English handwriting, Arabic script is joined (or cursive); there is no equivalent of the text you are reading now, where all the letters have separate forms with spaces between them.
▶ Arabic has no capital letters.
▶ Six of the 28 letters do not join to the letter that follows.
▶ Arabic letters have four possible forms, depending on whether these are written on their own, or come at the beginning, in the middle or at the end of a word. This is because the joining strokes between the letters, called ligatures, slightly affect the shape of the letters on either side.
▶ The three long vowels **aa**, **ii** and **uu** are shown in the script.
▶ The three short vowels **a**, **i**, and **u** are not shown in the script. For example, the word **bank** (borrowed from English) is written **b-n-k**.

The alphabet

First, don't expect to take all this in at once. You can always come back to it again later. Pace your learning to suit yourself!

Throughout *Beginners' Arabic*, we introduce a few Arabic letters in each unit and have given the forms of each letter on their own, at the beginning, in the middle and at the end of a word. If you look at the letters carefully, you will see that there are generally only two shapes.

The Arabic alphabet is given here in its traditional order. Letters that are non-joiners are marked with an asterisk (*).

THE ARABIC LETTERS

Name	Beginning	Middle	End	On its own	Pronunciation
alif*	ا	ـا	ـا	ا	a
baa'	بـ	ـبـ	ـب	ب	b
taa'	تـ	ـتـ	ـت	ت	t
thaa'	ثـ	ـثـ	ـث	ث	th
jiim	جـ	ـجـ	ـج	ج	j
Haa'	حـ	ـحـ	ـح	ح	H
khaa'	خـ	ـخـ	ـخ	خ	kh
daal*	د	ـد	ـد	د	d
dhaal*	ذ	ـذ	ـذ	ذ	dh
raa'*	ر	ـر	ـر	ر	r
zain*	ز	ـز	ـز	ز	z
siin	سـ	ـسـ	ـس	س	s
shiin	شـ	ـشـ	ـش	ش	sh
Saad	صـ	ـصـ	ـص	ص	S
Daad	ضـ	ـضـ	ـض	ض	D
Taa'	طـ	ـطـ	ـط	ط	T
Dhaa'	ظـ	ـظـ	ـظ	ظ	DH
:ain	عـ	ـعـ	ـع	ع	:
ghain	غـ	ـغـ	ـغ	غ	gh
faa'	فـ	ـفـ	ـف	ف	f
qaaf	قـ	ـقـ	ـق	ق	q
kaaf	كـ	ـكـ	ـك	ك	k
laam	لـ	ـلـ	ـل	ل	l
miim	مـ	ـمـ	ـم	م	m
nuun	نـ	ـنـ	ـن	ن	n
haa'	هـ	ـهـ	ـه	ه	h
waaw*	و	ـو	ـو	و	w
yaa'	يـ	ـيـ	ي	ي	y

When we say the letter comes at the end, we mean that it is final after a joining letter. If the letter before it is a non-joiner, then the separate form is used. If you look closely, you can see that many final and separate letters are stretched out, or have a 'flourish' after them.

This is what **baa'** looks like in its four forms – can you see the similarities?

Beginning	Middle	End	On its own
ـب	ـبـ	ـب	ب

You can see that the basic form is the hook with a dot under it, the middle shape has joining strokes before and after it, and the final form has an elongation or flourish.

There is one combination consonant, called **laam-alif**. This is used when this series of letters occurs, and it is a non-joiner:

Name	Beginning	Middle/End	On its own	Pronunciation
laam-alif	لا	ـلا	لا	laa

There is a letter called **taa' marbuuTah**, literally a 'bound' or 'tied' **taa'**. This is the Arabic feminine ending which occurs at the end of words, so it only ever has two forms: ending (after joiners) and on its own (after non-joiners). It sounds like 'ah', which is how we have transcribed it. So look out for words in this book ending in **-ah** – many of these will be feminine nouns or adjectives.

Ending	On its own
ـة	ة

If you look at it carefully, you will see that it is a **haa'** with the two dots of the **taa'** added. Sometimes **taa' marbuuTah** is 'untied' and regains its **taa'** sound. But don't worry about this; we only mention it here because you will come across it from time to time and may wonder what it is. For example:

sayyáarah (*car*) becomes **sayyáarat al-mudíir** (*the manager's car*)

tádhkarah (*ticket*) becomes **tádhkarat dhiháab w iyáab** (*a return ticket*)

VOWELS

The long vowels are expressed by the three letters **alif**, **waaw** and **yaa'**.

ا **alif** almost always expresses the vowel '*aa*' as in *calm*.

و **waaw** expresses the vowel '*oo*' as in *cool*, and can be the consonant *w* as in English *wish*.

ي **yaa'** expresses the vowel '*ee*' as in *keep*, and can be the consonant *y* as in English *yes*.

In Arabic writing, short vowels such as the *a* in *bat*, rather than the longer *a* in *calm*, are not usually marked except in the Holy Qur'an, schoolchildren's textbooks and ancient classical poetry. You will be introduced to the short vowels in the final unit of this book. Don't worry – rdng wtht shrt vwls snt s dffclt s y mght thnk!

Basically, it is better to think of the Arabic script as handwriting, since it is always cursive, no matter how it is produced. Because of this, calligraphy has become a highly developed art and so there are more variations in the form of letters than you would find in English. In *Beginners' Arabic* we will help you to recognize the Arabic script, rather than to learn to write with it, and there are fuller descriptions of all the letters in each unit. Arabic writing is fun to read. Look on it as an art form!

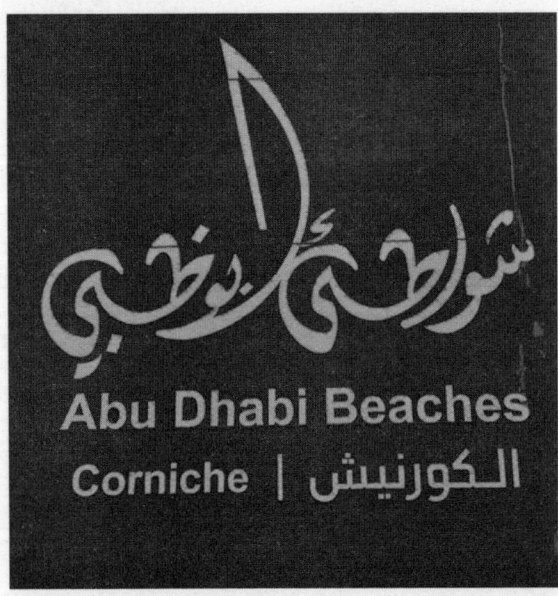

Pronunciation

Transliteration

Transliteration means expressing a language that uses a different writing system (like Arabic) in letters and symbols based on the Roman alphabet. There is no standard way of doing this, and we have tried to keep the system used in *Beginners' Arabic* as simple as possible.

The most important feature of a transliteration system is that it has an equivalent for every sound in the target language. This is different from conventional spelling. So, for example, in English the letter *s* has totally different sounds in the two words *loafs* and *loaves*, and the same *s* sound used in *loafs* can be spelled differently, as in *mince*. *Beginners' Arabic* is more or less restricted to the English alphabet, and we use capital letters to distinguish between Arabic sounds that seem related to non-Arabic speakers. For instance, Arabic has two sorts of **t**, which are distinguished like this: **tiin** means *figs*, and **Tiin** means *mud*. There is a full explanation of how to pronounce these sounds in the next section.

The Arabic sounds

The letters are given in standard Roman alphabet order, not in traditional Arabic order, so you can find the sounds more easily. The sound corresponding with the transliteration used in this book is given first, followed by the Arabic name for the letter. An example of the letter in an Arabic word is then followed by the English translation of the word.

We have divided the pronunciation guide into three groups:
▶ Group 1: Sounds that are more or less as in English.
▶ Group 2: Sounds that we don't have in English, but which are found in other European languages.
▶ Group 3: Sounds that are specific to Arabic.

GROUP 1

00.01

b	baa'	as in **baab** door
d	daal	as in **dars** lesson
dh	dhaal	as in **dháalik** that
f	faa'	as in **filfil** pepper
h	haa'	as in **húwwa** he
j	jiim	as in **jadíid** new
k	kaaf	as in **kabíir** big
l	laam	as in **laa** not, and it sometimes has a duller sound, as in English alter
m	miim	as in **múmkin** possible
n	nuun	as in **nuur** light
s	siin	as in **símsim** sesame
sh	shiin	as in **sharíi:ah** sharia (Islamic law)
t	taa'	as in **táajir** merchant
th	thaa'	as in **thaláathah** three
w	waaw	as in **wáaHid** one
y	yaa'	as in **yoom** day
z	zaay	as in **zooj** husband

GROUP 2

00.02

r	raa'	as in **rájul** man. This is the trilled r of Scottish very ('verry'), and common in Italian and Spanish (Parma, Barcelona).
gh	ghain	as in **gharb** west; similar to the r of Parisian French
kh	khaa'	as in **kháarij** outside; like the sound of ch in Scottish loch

GROUP 3

00.03

These sounds are specific to Arabic. To pronounce them requires practice and it is best to listen to Arabic speakers if you can.

S, **T**, **D**, **DH**. With the exception of **H** (see below), the capitalized consonants are pronounced in a similar way to their small letter versions **s**, **t**, **d** and **dh**, except that the tongue is pressed down into a spoon shape and the sound is more forceful. These sounds have an effect on any surrounding vowels, which makes them sound more hollow. A rough (British) English equivalent is the difference in the *a* as in *Sam* and in *palm*.

S	**Saad**	as in **Saghíir** *small*
T	**Taa'**	as in **Táalib** *student*
D	**Daad**	as in **Dayf** *guest*
DH	**DHaa'**	as in **DHuhr** *noon*
:	**:ain**	as in **:ámal** *work*. You will find that what is normally called gagging in English is actually a restriction in the deep part of the throat. If you begin to gag and then immediately relax the muscles in order to release the airstream from the lungs, you will have produced a perfect **:ain**.
H	**Haa'**	as in **Hajj** *pilgrimage*. Pronounced in exactly the same way as **:ain**, except that, instead of completely closing the muscles referred to above, they are just constricted and the air is allowed to escape. The only time English speakers come near to a (weakish) **H** is when they breathe on their glasses before cleaning them. Both **:ain** and **Haa'** should always be pronounced with the mouth fairly wide open (say '*ah*').
'	**hamza**	as in **'ámal** *hope*. The **hamzah** or glottal stop occurs in English between words pronounced deliberately and emphatically (e.g. *She* (pause) *is* (pause) *awful!*), but is probably more familiar as the Cockney pronunciation of *t* or *tt* as in *bottle*. This sound is different from the **:ain**, and the difference affects the meaning. For instance, **'ámal** means *hope*, but **:amal** means *work*.
q	**qaaf**	as in **qaríib** *near*. Officially pronounced as a 'back of the throat' English *c* or *k*, and not related to the *qu* in English. A rough equivalent is the pronunciation of the letter *c* in (British) English *calm*.

LOCAL VARIATIONS

Arabic speakers from different regions throughout the Gulf pronounce some letters differently, so you may hear the following variations:

j	pronounced as **y**, e.g. **dajáaj** (*chicken*) = **dayáay**, and also as **g** or **j** as in French *Jacques*
dh and **DH**	pronounced as **d** or **z**
D	pronounced as **DH** in much of the Gulf
k	sometimes pronounced as **ch** in parts of the Gulf, e.g. **baakir** (*tomorrow*), or **baachir**
q*	pronounced as **g** in much of the Gulf

*In *Beginners' Arabic* we have introduced words containing **q** in both their Gulf and MSA forms, e.g. **garíib/qaríib** (*near*) and **suug/suuq** (*market*), but have listed them under **q** in the Vocabulary section (with both forms). In the **Go further** script sections, however, we have used the standard Arabic **q** transliteration only to help you link the sound with the written letter **qaaf**, i.e. **suuq** (*market*) appears only as **suuq** and not as **suug**.

VOWELS

00.04 There are only five common vowel sounds, three of which occur both long and short. These have been transcribed as follows:

aa	as in **tháalith** *third*, a long emphatic *a* as in the word *and* in: 'Did he really eat a whole chicken?' 'Yes, <u>and</u> he ate a steak as well!'
a	as in **ábadan** *never*, roughly as in *hat*
ii	as in **kabíir** *big*, as in *leave* and French *livre*
i	as in **jíbin** *cheese*, like *big*
uu	as in **filúus** *money*, like *rude*, French *vous*, or German *Schule*
u	as in **buldáan** *countries*, like *put* (never as in *cup*)
oo	as in **tilifóon** *telephone*, or French *beau*
ai	as in **bait** *house*, like *wait*

You also hear this last pair of vowels:

ay	as in **dubáy** *Dubai*, like *aye*

DOUBLED CONSONANTS

00.05 These must be pronounced clearly twice in Arabic. Imagine a sort of hyphen between them. One example should make this clear:

Hamaam means *pigeons*

Hammaam means *bath* or *bathroom*.

STRESS

00.06 The best way to learn where the stress in each new word falls is to listen to the audio as often as you can, and practice saying the words and phrases out loud. Listening to Arabic speakers and Arab media as much as possible will also help you 'get your ear in.'

One simple general rule, however, is that if a word contains a long vowel (**aa**, **ii** or **uu**), the stress falls on this; and if there is more than one (long vowel), the stress falls on the one nearest the end of the word:

makáatib but **makaatíib**

The stress will be on the last long syllable before a vowel ending.

To help you get used to where the stress falls, the stressed syllables of words have been marked with an accent, **á**, **áa**, etc., in the first seven units.

PRONUNCIATION OF 'AL-' (*THE*)

In Arabic writing, **al-** (*the*) never stands alone as it does in English. It is always attached to another word. Although it never changes in writing, **al-** has one peculiarity. If the word it is joined to begins with one of the following fourteen letters:

t, th, d, dh, r, z, s, sh, S, D, T, DH, l, n

the 'l' (**laam**) of **al-** is dropped in speech and the first letter of the word it is attached to is clearly doubled.

These particular letters are known as Sun letters, simply because the word **shams** (*sun*) begins with **shiin**, which is one of them. The remaining letters are known as Moon letters because **qámar** (*moon*) begins with **qaaf**, which is not a Sun letter.

For example, we write and say **al-kuwáit** (**kaaf** is not a Sun letter), but we write **al-sháarjah** and say **ash-sháarjah** (**shiin** is a Sun letter). You can see that in **ash-sháarjah** the **shiin** is doubled. We have shown this in the transliteration in this book. It is an important point of pronunciation and you must pronounce the doubled versions of the letters listed above clearly. With practice, you will soon be doing this without thinking.

This photograph shows the inconsistent transliteration of Arabic signs. The correct pronunciation is **as-suuq** or **as-suug** in Gulf Arabic.

Look at the following words and phrases. Do the words following al- begin with Sun or Moon letters? (Note: there are two answers for d and f.)

   a SabáaH al-kháir (*good morning*)

   b SabáaH an-núur (*good morning to you too*)

   c al-kuwáit (*Kuwait*)

   d ar-rub: al-kháali (*the Empty Quarter*)

   e as-sa:udíyyah (*Saudi*)

   f ash-sharq al-áwsaT (*the Middle East*)

   g ash-shamáal (*the North*)

   h al-khalíij (*the Gulf*)

   i as-saláamu :aláikum (*hello*)

   j al-imaaráat (*the Emirates*)

00.07 **Listen and repeat.**

1

In this unit you will learn how to:
» say *hello* and *goodbye*.
» use common greetings.
» introduce yourself and others.
» say where you're from.
» ask someone where they are from.

áhlan wa sáhlan!

My progress tracker →

DAY / DATE	🎧	🎤	📖	💬
	○	○	○	○
	○	○	○	○
	○	○	○	○
	○	○	○	○
	○	○	○	○
	○	○	○	○

The Gulf

The Arabic you will learn in this book is called Gulf Arabic, the language spoken in **al-khalíij** (*the Gulf*). This region includes the land that extends from **al-:iráaq** (*Iraq*) in **ash-shamáal** (*the North*) to **al-yáman** (*Yemen*) in **al-janúub** (*the South*) and from **al-mámlakah al-:arabíyyah as-sa:udíyyah** (*the Kingdom of Saudi Arabia*), also known simply as **as-sa:udíyyah**, in the West to **:umáan** (*Oman*) in the East.

The Gulf is an important region in **ash-sharg al-áwsaT** (*the Middle East*). **:árabi** (*Arabic*) – or more formally **al-lúghah al-:arabíyyah** (*the Arabic language*), which is spoken in **al-khalíij** – varies slightly from country to country, but the language introduced in this book is widely understood throughout the region. From the skyscrapers and opulent malls of **dubáy** (*Dubai*) to the desert wilderness of **ar-rub: al-kháali** (*the Empty Quarter*), **al-khalíij** is truly a region of contrasts with something for everyone.

What is the Arabic word for *language*?

Vocabulary builder

GREETINGS AND GOODBYES

In Arabic, it is very important to be able to greet people, to reply appropriately when someone greets you, and to say goodbye.

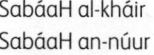

01.01 Look at these words and phrases, then listen and practice these sounds by imitating the pronunciation of the speakers.

SabáaH al-kháir	*good morning*
SabáaH an-núur	*good morning* (only used in reply to **SabáaH al-kháir**)
masáa' al-kháir	*good afternoon/evening*
masáa' an-núur	*good afternoon/evening* (reply to **masáa' al-kháir**)
má:a s-saláamah	*goodbye* (reply is the same)

> **PRONUNCIATION TIP**
> Remember to pronounce the stress where marked!

NEW EXPRESSIONS

01.02 Note the meaning of these Arabic expressions and try to pronounce them with the marked stresses.

ána ...	*I ...*
ínta	*you* (to a man)
ínti	*you* (to a woman)
ísm-i ...	*My name ...* (lit. *name-my ...*)
aish ísm-ak?	*What's your name?*
	(lit. *what name-your?*)
	(to a man)
aish ísm-ich?	*What's your name?*
	(lit. *what name-your?*)
	(to a woman)
kaif Háal-ak?	*How are you?*
	(lit. *how condition-your?*)
	(to a man)
kaif Háal-ich?	*How are you?*
	(lit. *how condition-your?*)
	(to a woman)
al-Hámdu li-l-láah	*fine* (lit. *thanks to God*)
bi-kháir	*well*
wa	*and*
wa ínta?	*And you?*
	(to a man)
wa ínti?	*And you?*
	(to a woman)
ínta min wain?	*Where are you from?*
	(lit. *you from where?*)
	(to a man)
ínti min wain?	*Where are you from?*
	(lit. *you from where?*)
	(to a woman)
ána min dubáy	*I (am) from Dubai*

> **PRONUNCIATION TIP**
>
> Some word endings differ when speaking to a man or a woman. Make sure your endings are clear so as not to offend!

4

Hiwáar 1 *Conversation 1*

01.03 *At a business meeting in Abu Dhabi, Mohammed talks to Laila, another participant. Listen first, then answer the question.*

1 What time of day is it?

Mohammed	SabáaH al-kháir.
Laila	SabáaH an-núur. aish ísm-ak?
Mohammed	ána ísm-i muHámmad. wa ínti, aish ísm-ich?
Laila	ána ísm-i laila.
Mohammed	kaif Háal-ich?
Laila	al-Hámdu li-l-láah, bi-kháir. wa ínta, kaif Háal-ak?
Mohammed	al-Hámdu li-l-láah.
Laila	ínta min wain?
Mohammed	ána min dubáy. wa ínti?
Laila	ána min ábu DHábi.

> **AL-HÁMDU LI-L-LÁAH**
>
> The expression **al-Hámdu li-l-láah** never changes and is used in many situations. Even if they are seriously unwell, many people will still use this phrase when asked how they are!

2 What do you think? Read the conversation and answer the following questions.

  a Does Mohammed know Laila?

  b Where does Mohammed come from?

3 Match the Arabic to its correct English meaning.

a	SabáaH al-kháir	**1**	My name is
b	aish ísm-ich?	**2**	fine (lit. thanks to God)
c	ána ísm-i	**3**	Good morning.
d	kaif Háal-ak?	**4**	What's your name?
e	al-Hámdu li-l-láah	**5**	How are you?

4 01.03 **Now listen again line by line and try to imitate the speakers. Pay careful attention to the pronunciation and notice where the stress is on each word.**

Language discovery

a Look at these phrases. What do you notice about the way *is* is said in Arabic?

aish ísm-ak?

ána ísm-i muHámmad

ána min dubáy

b Two different words for *you* are used in the conversation: **ínta** and **ínti**. Why?

c Find the word **ism-** throughout the conversation. How many different endings does it have, and what are these?

1 *IS* AND *ARE*

In Arabic there is no equivalent of the verb *to be* in the present tense. English sentences containing the words *is* or *are* are formed in Arabic as follows:

ána ísm-i joon	*My name is John.* (lit. *I name-my John.*)
aish ísm-ak?	*What is your name?* (lit. *What name-your?*)
kaif Háal-ak?	*How are you?* (lit. *How condition-your?*)
ínta min amríika?	*Are you from America?* (lit. *You from America?*)

al-Hiin door-ak!   *Now your turn!*

How would you say what your name is in Arabic?

2 PRONOUNS: *I* AND *YOU* (TO A MAN AND TO A WOMAN)

A pronoun is a word that refers to a person or a thing, such as *I, you, he, she* or *it*. Instead of saying *Selena is from England*, we can use a pronoun to replace the name *Selena*, and say *She is from England*.

The word **ána** always means *I*, whatever your gender. However, in Arabic there is a very clear distinction when saying *you* to a man or woman. To say *you* to a man use **ínta**, and to a woman say **ínti**.

ínta min al-kuwáit?	*(Are) you from Kuwait?* (to a man)
laa, ána min al-imaaráat.	*No, I (am) from the Emirates.*
ínti min ustráalya?	*(Are) you from Australia?* (to a woman)
ná:am, ána min sídni!	*Yes, I('m) from Sydney!*

TIP			
laa	*no*	**ná:am** (also **áywa**)	*yes*

6

al-Hiin door-ak! *Now your turn!*

So, how do you say *I am from Australia*?

3 POSSESSIVE PRONOUNS: *MY* AND *YOUR*

Possessives describe *who* or *what* something belongs to. In English we use the words *my, your, his* and *hers*. To say *my* and *your* in Arabic we add an ending (called a suffix) to the person or thing being possessed. The endings in the conversation you have just heard are:

-i	*my*	**ísm-i** *my name* (lit. *name-my*)
-ak	*your* (to a man)	**ísm-ak** *your name* (lit. *name-your*) (to a man)
-ich	*your* (to a woman)	**ísm-ich** *your name* (lit. *name-your*) (to a woman)

> **PRONUNCIATION TIP**
> The feminine pronoun ending **-ich** is the most common pronunciation in the Gulf, but you may also hear **-ik** or even **-ish**, as in **kaif Háal-ish** (*How are you?* to a woman).

PRACTICE 1

1 Complete each sentence by adding the correct word(s).

> **gáTar   Háal-ich   ísm-i   min**

a ána _____ jaimz (*James*).
b ána _____ iskutláanda.
c áHmad min _____.
d kaif _____?

> **TIP**
> iskutláanda   Scotland
> gáTar (qáTar)   Qatar

2 First read, then add the missing Arabic words. Don't forget to check whether the endings are masculine or feminine!

Aliyah	masáa' al-kháir.
Jamal	masáa' an-núur. aish ísm-_____?
Aliyah	ána ísm-_____ :alya. wa _____, aish ism-_____?
Jamal	ána ísm-i jmáal.
Aliyah	kaif Háal-_____?
Jamal	al-Hámdu li-l-láah, bi-kháir. wa _____?

3 Complete each sentence by adding the correct word from those supplied in the box. Careful – there are two words you won't need!

> ísm-ak   kaif   ínta   ísm-i
> Háal-ich   ána   min

a ána _____ záinab.
b aish _____?
c _____ ísm-i Hámad.
d _____ min wain?
e kaif _____?

Listen and understand

 1 01.04 **Listen to these people telling you their names and where they are from. Match the correct place to each person.**

a Khalid   1 London, England
b Ahmed al-Qasimi   2 Abu Dhabi in the Emirates
c James Smith   3 Oman
d Dalya   4 New York
e Karen McGregor   5 Saudi Arabia
f Zainab al-Loozi   6 Bahrain

 2 01.05 **Listen to these speakers, then say if they are talking to a man or a woman.**

a m/f   b m/f   c m/f
d m/f   e m/f   f m/f

Vocabulary

01.06 Look at these words and phrases, then listen and practice by imitating the pronunciation of the speakers.

as-saláamu :aláikum	*hello* (lit. *peace be on you*)
wa :aláikum as-saláam	*hello* (lit. *and on you be peace* – only used in reply to as-saláamu :aláikum)
áhlan wa sáhlan	*hello/welcome*
áhlan bii-k/bii-ch	*hello/welcome* (m/f) (reply to **áhlan wa sáhlan**)

> **PRONUNCIATION TIP**
> The **-a** of **wa** (*and*) often slides into the next word if the next word starts with a vowel, so **wa :aláikum as-saláam** becomes **w :aláikum as-saláam**. Try it for yourself!

Hiwáar 2 *Conversation 2*

01.07 *Mohammed and Laila meet again later. Mohammed introduces his friends Mark and Sara.*

1 Read as you listen. Which countries are Mark and Sara from?

Laila	as-saláamu :aláikum.
Mohammed	w :aláikum as-saláam. kaif Háal-ich yaa láila?
Laila	al Hámdu li-l-lah.
Mohammed	háadha mark, húwwa min lándan fii ingiltarra. wa háadhi sáarah, híyya min amríika.
Laila	áhlan wa sáhlan.
Mark and Sara	áhlan bii-ch.

> **YAA**
> In Arabic, the word **yaa** is usually used when addressing someone by name.

2 Which city is Mark from?

3 Match the Arabic to the English.

a	híyya min amríika	**1**	hello/welcome
b	háadha	**2**	this (f)
c	húwwa min lándan	**3**	she (is) from America
d	háadhi	**4**	this (m)
e	áhlan wa sáhlan	**5**	he (is) from London

Language discovery

1 Find the words **húwwa** and **híyya** in the conversation – which means *he* and which means *she*?

2 Mohammed used the words **háadha** and **háadhi** to introduce Mark and Sara. What do you think these words mean?

1 MORE PRONOUNS – *HE* AND *SHE*

You have already learned how to say *I*, and *you* to a man and a woman. Here are two more pronouns: *he* and *she*.

húwwa	he	mark min lándan → húwwa min lándan	He (is) from London.
híyya	she	sáarah min amríika → híyya min amríika	She (is) from America.

2 HOW TO SAY *THIS*

In Arabic, the words **háadha** and **háadhi** are also pronouns and mean *this*.

háadha   *this* (masculine)   **háadhi**   *this* (feminine)

They can also be used to make sentences since there is no verb *to be* in Arabic.

háadha fáysal   *This (is) Faisal.*

háadhi náadiya   *This (is) Nadia.*

PRACTICE 2

1 Complete each sentence with either **húwwa** or **híyya** to say where each person is from.

   a muHámmad: _____ min al-baHráin.

   b ánya: _____ min briTáaniya.

   c fáaTimah: _____ min ash-shárjah.

   d jaak: _____ min faránsa.

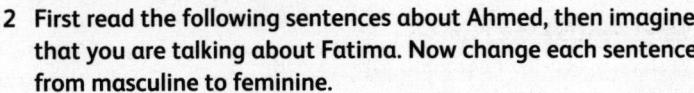 2 First read the following sentences about Ahmed, then imagine that you are talking about Fatima. Now change each sentence from masculine to feminine.

   a háadha áHmad.

   b húwwa min ábu DHábi?

   c laa, húwwa min gáTar.

3 01.08 **Listen to these speakers introduce their friends. Which speakers are male and which are female?**

a háadha iqbáal
b háadha tamíim
c háadha :áadil
d háadhi jamíilah
e háadhi sáarah
f háadha imrán

4 01.09 **Now introduce the following people and say where each is from.**

Example: a háadha málik, húwwa min másqat.

a málik (m) – másqat (*Muscat*)
b náasir (m) – jid-dah (*Jeddah*)
c híbah (f) – al-yáman (*Yemen*)
d sofia (f) – isbáanya (*Spain*)

Go further

READING ARABIC

The Arabic word for *the* is **al-** and it is written like this in Arabic:

الـ   **al-**   *the*

It is always attached to the word that follows it and is written with two letters, **alif** (ا) and **laam** (ل). **al-** is easy to recognize, as it always comes at the beginning of a word: الـ ... as you can see in the following examples. Remember, Arabic script is read from right to left!

| الخليج | **al-khalíij** | *the* Gulf |
| اليمن | **al-yáman** | Yemen |

In English the names of some countries have *the* in front of them, such as the Netherlands and the USA. It is the same in Arabic but there are more of them, and they aren't always translated in English, as in Yemen. For example, **al-baHráin** (lit. *the Bahrain*) is just known as Bahrain in English.

> **WHAT'S IN A NAME?**
> Do you know what **al-baHráin** means? **báHar**, or **baHr**, means *sea* and **-ain** means *two* of anything – so when you add them together **al-baHráin** means *the two seas*, which describes its setting in the Gulf beautifully.

> **PRONUNCIATION TIP**
> Remember that if the name of the country begins with a Sun letter, the **l** of **al-** disappears, and the first letter must be doubled! (See Pronunciation.)

The letters **alif** and **laam** also appear separately. **alif** often has a small figure called a **hamza** (which looks like a backwards figure two) above or below it. If it is above the **alif** it makes it sound like **a** as in the name **Ahmed**, or like **u** as in **ukht** (*sister*). If the **hamza** is below the **alif**, it sounds like **i**, as in the word **ingiltárra**. **alif** is one of the six non-joiners, i.e. it doesn't join to the following letter. Here are **alif** and **laam** in their different positions.

end of a word	middle of a word	start of a word	on its own
سينما **síinma** *cinema*	سارة **sáarah** *Sara* (girl's name)	أحمد **áHmad** *Ahmed* (boy's name) إنجليزي **inglíizi** *English* أخت **ukht** *sister*	ا **alif** أ إ
مول **mool** *mall*	خليج **khalíij** *gulf*	ليمون **laimóon** *lemon*	ل **laam**

Did you spot the laam in the middle of the word khalíij?

1 **Find three countries in the following list that begin with ... الـ (al-) (*the*) in Arabic.**

	Arabic	English
1	الكويت	Kuwait
2	قطر	Qatar
3	العراق	Iraq
4	السودان	Sudan
5	عمان	Oman

2 01.10 **First listen to the pronunciation of these Arab countries, then practice saying them by imitating the speakers.**

as-sudáan   al-:iráaq

:umáan   al-baHráin

al-yáman   qáTar

> **TIP**
> You will find a range of countries in the core vocabulary.

3 **The word … الـ (al-) is very common in street names. Can you find it in these Dubai street signs?**

> **PRONUNCIATION TIP**
> The correct pronunciation of **al Safa** would be **aS-Safa** since **Saad** is a Sun letter.

Test yourself

1 **Give your own response to each greeting/question, taking care with your pronunciation.**
   a as-saláamu :aláikum
   b masáa' al-kháir
   c aish ísm-ak/ísm-ich?
   d ínta/ínti min wain?
   e má:a s-saláamah

2 01.11 **What is the missing word in each phrase?**
   a as-saláamu _____
   b áhlan _____ sáhlan
   c húwwa _____ briTáaniya
   d _____ ísm-i maHmóod (Mahmoud)
   e _____ an-núur
   f _____ Háal-ak?
   g _____ fiyóona smiith

3 **What questions would you ask to get these replies?**
   a Speaker 1: _____
      Speaker 2: ána ísm-i náadiya.
   b Speaker 1: _____
      Speaker 2: ána ísm-i Hámad.
   c Speaker 1: _____(to a man)
      Speaker 2: al-Hámdu li-l-láah, w ínta?

SELF CHECK

I CAN . . .

○	... say *hello* and *goodbye*.
○	... use common greetings.
○	... introduce myself and others.
○	... say where I'm from.
○	... ask someone where they are from.

2

In this unit you will learn how to:
» state your nationality.
» say what languages you speak.
» recognize and use numbers 0–10.
» ask for and give phone numbers.
» ask for someone on the phone.

ta-takállam :árabi?

My progress tracker →

DAY / DATE	🎧	🎤	📖	💬
	○	○	○	○
	○	○	○	○
	○	○	○	○
	○	○	○	○
	○	○	○	○
	○	○	○	○
	○	○	○	○

Arabic numbers

Any attempt to speak **:árabi** (*Arabic*) is met with delight. People are very interested in visitors who can speak even a few words of their language, so being able to say a little about yourself in Arabic, such as your **jinsíyyah** (*nationality*), will be well received.

During the Middle Ages the torch of Classical learning was passed to Western scholars by the Arab world, which had introduced the simpler decimal system that we use today, and spread the concept of **Sífir** (*zero* or *cipher*). There are many other words used in English, such as *algebra* and *algorithm*, that are Arabic in origin. It is useful to know Arabic numerals when you are out and about in the Gulf to help you deal confidently with such things as prices and phone numbers.

Although the word **tilifóon** is commonly used, mobile phones are also called **háatif** (the original word for *phone*) or **maHmoul** (the Arabic word for something portable or that you can carry). Sometimes these two terms make a compound word. But the most common word in current usage throughout the Arabic-speaking world is **jawwaal** (something that roams or is nomadic). This also is often used for other mobile devices beyond phones.

Look at these Arabic numbers. Can you work out what they are?

٩   ٣   ١   ٢

Vocabulary builder

AL-JINSIYYÁAT WAL-LUGHÁAT
NATIONALITIES AND LANGUAGES

 1 02.01 **Listen and match each nationality in Arabic to its English translation.**

a sá:udi	**1**	French
b imaráati	**2**	British
c brazíili	**3**	American
d briTáani	**4**	Brazilian
e faránsi	**5**	Saudi
f amríiki	**6**	Emirati
g táailándi	**7**	Thai

 Now cover up the Arabic. Can you say the Arabic words again without looking?

2 What are these languages in English?

a :árabi	**c** isbáani
b inglíizi	**d** faránsi/faransáawi

> **AL-LÚGHAH AL-:ARABÍYYAH**
> The formal name for the Arabic language is **al-lúghah al-:arabíyyah**. As **al-lúghah** is a feminine word, the word describing it must also be feminine, but most often people just use the word **:árabi** (*Arabic*). Similarly, English becomes **inglíizi**.

NEW EXPRESSIONS

 02.02 **Can you add the missing meanings in English?**

min fáDHl-ak	*please* (to a man)
min fáDHl-ich	*please* (to a woman)
shúkran	*thank you*
:áfwan	*you're welcome* (reply to above)
shwáyya shwáyya	*slowly* (lit. *a little a little*)
:an idhn-ak	*excuse me* (to a man)

:an ídhn-ich	*excuse me* (to a woman)
a-takállam :árabi	*I speak* _____
maa a-takállam inglíizi	*I don't speak* _____
ta-takállam inglíizi?	*Do you* (to a man) *speak* _____?
ta-takállam-íin inglíizi?	*Do you* (to a woman) *speak* _____?
wáajid (*also* wáayid) zain	*very good/very well*
shwáyya	*a little*
bass	*only/enough*
ínta baHráin-i?	*Are you Bahraini?* (m)
ána miSr-íyyah	*I am Egyptian* (f)
áasif	*I'm sorry* (man speaking)
áasfah	*I'm sorry* (woman speaking)

Hiwáar 1 *Conversation 1*

02.03 *In Abu Dhabi, Lauren and Alex get talking to Nasser. First listen and follow the text. Then answer the question.*

1 What nationality is Nasser?

Lauren	:an ídhn-ak, ta-takállam inglíizi?
Nasser	laa, áasif, a-takállam :árabi bass.
	ínti ingliz-íyyah?
Lauren	laa, ána amrik-íyyah. w ínta?
Nasser	ána imaráat-i. ta-takállam-íin :árabi wáajid zain!
Lauren	(*laughs*) laa, laa, shwáyya bass. háadha aliks, húwwa briTáan-i.
Nasser	áhlan wa sáhlan.
Alex	áhlan biik.

> **BASS**
>
> **bass** is a very useful little word with a number of meanings. Depending on the context, it can mean *just*, *enough*, *stop* or *but*.

al-Hiin door-ak! *Now your turn!*

**You are reversing your car when someone behind you shouts *bass!*
What should you do?**

   a go slower
   b go faster
   c hit the brakes immediately

2 Read the conversation again, then answer these questions.
   a What does Lauren ask Nasser first?
   b What languages does Nasser speak?
   c What does Nasser say about Lauren's Arabic?
   d What is the Arabic word for *no*?
   e Who is American?
   f Who is British?

 3 02.03 **Listen again, then decide which statements are true (T) and which are false (F).**
   a Nasser speaks English.
   b Lauren is American.
   c Nasser is Qatari.

 4 02.03 **Listen again, this time taking the part of Lauren.**

Language discovery

1 Look at these expressions from the conversation. Why do they use different endings for their nationalities?
   Nasser: ána imaráat-i
   Lauren: ána amrik-íyyah

2 What is the Arabic for these phrases?
   a I speak
   b you speak (m)
   c you speak (f)

1 NATIONALITY ADJECTIVES

In Arabic, words describing nationality are usually formed by adding a masculine or feminine ending to the name of the country. For most nationalities you add:

-i for a man   **-íyyah** for a woman

gáTar *Qatar* → **gáTar-i** *Qatari* (m) or **gaTar-íyyah** *Qatari* (f)

If the name of a country ends in **-a** or **-ah**, this is left off before the ending is added:

briTáaniya *Britain* → **briTáan-i/briTan-íyyah** *British*

faránsa *France* → **faráns-i/farans-íyyah** *French*

But use:

ingiltárra *England* → **inglíiz-i/ingliz-íyyah** *English*

If the place name in Arabic has **al-** (*the*) in front of it, this is left out.

al-baHráin *Bahrain* → **baHráin-i/baHrain-íyyah** *Bahraini*

as-sudáan *Sudan* → **sudáan-i/sudaan-íyyah** *Sudani*

2 I SPEAK, YOU SPEAK

In English, verb forms are all the same, regardless of the subject (e.g. *I speak, you speak*) with the exception of *he/she speaks*. In Arabic, the verb changes slightly, depending on the subject.

(ána) a-takállam	*I speak*
(ínta) ta-takállam	*you* (m) *speak*
(ínti) ta-takallam-íin	*you* (f) *speak*

> **PRONOUNS**
> Pronouns are not always used, since the verb form indicates the subject. You will learn more about this in Unit 3.

PRACTICE 1

1 Are these nationalities masculine or feminine?

    a imaráat-i

    b alman-íyyah

    c ustráal-i

    d ingliz-íyyah

    e baHrain-íyyah

    f faráns-i

    g kuwáit-i

    h irland-íyyah

    i hind-ii

    j Sin-iyyah

>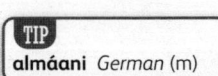
> **TIP**
> **almáani** *German* (m)

2 Make each sentence feminine, as shown in the example. Remember to change the pronouns (*you, he*) where necessary.

    Example: a ána ingliz-íiyyah min lándan.

    a ána inglíiz-i, min lándan.

    b ínta iTáal-i?

    c húwwa :umáan-i.

    d húwwa sudáan-i.

    e ána briTáan-i, min iskutlánda.

    f ínta gáTar-i?

3 Now translate the sentences in exercise 2 into English.

4 Who's talking? Look at the following phrases, then match them to the correct image.

1   2   3

a a-takállam inglíizi
b a-takallam faránsi
c a-takállam :árabi

5 Complete the conversation between Khalid and Tomas by adding the most appropriate words from those supplied.
Speak out loud.

shwáyya	inglíiz-i	wáajid	zain
laa, laa	laa	ínta	min

Khalid   _____ amríik-i?
Tomas   laa, ána _____
Khalid   ínta _____ lándan?
Tomas   _____, ána min máanshistr!
Khalid   ta-takállam :árabi _____!
Tomas   laa, _____ bass.

Listen and understand

1 02.04 First listen, then repeat these useful expressions out loud. Do this several times until you are confident with your pronunciation.

a min fáDHlak   **d** :an ídhnik
b shúkran   **e** wáajid zain
c :áfwan   **f** shwáyya

2 02.05 Listen to each person stating their nationality. Who's talking? What are their nationalities?

a _____
b _____
c _____
d _____
e _____
f _____

3 Look at the pictures in exercise 2 again, then state the nationalities in Arabic. Start with 'ána ...'

22

AL-A:ADÁAD · – ١· *NUMBERS 0–10*

02.06 Listen twice to the speaker count from zero to 10, then repeat after the speaker.

Arabic numeral	Arabic pronunciation	English
·	Sífir	0
١	wáaHid	1
٢	ithnáin	2
٣	thaláathah	3
٤	árba:ah	4
٥	khámsah	5
٦	síttah	6
٧	sáb:ah	7
٨	thamáan(i)yah	8
٩	tís(a):ah	9
١·	:ásharah	10

> **ARABIC NUMBERS**
> In Arabic, numbers are written from left to right in the same direction as English, e.g. ١٩٢٤ = 1924. Some countries now use the same form we use (1, 2, 3, etc.) and this practice is spreading.

NEW EXPRESSIONS

02.07 Look at these phrases, then listen and practice by imitating the pronunciation of the speakers.

kam rágam tilifóon-ak/-ich?	*What (is) your phone number?*
rágam tilifóon-i ...	*My phone number is ...*
márrah tháaniyah	*again (lit. a second time)*

> **PRONUNCIATION TIP**
> Be aware that you will hear both **rágam** and **ráqam**, and even **ragm** or **raqm**.

ASKING FOR PEOPLE ON THE PHONE

To ask for someone on the phone, simply say (the name of the person you want) **mawjúud?** This is the standard way of asking if someone is available. As **mawjúud** is an adjective describing a person or thing, it agrees in gender so if the person you want is a woman, it becomes **mawjúud-ah**.

:abd al-:azíiz mawjúud?	*(Is) Abdel Aziz there (lit. present)?*
áywa, húwwa mawjúud.	*Yes, he (is) here.*
fáaTimah mawjúud-ah?	*(Is) Fatimah there?*
laa, híyya muu mawjúud-ah.	*No, she is not here.*

> **TIP**
> The word **muu** is used to make a noun or adjective negative.

Hiwáar 2 *Conversation 2*

🎧 02.08 *Mohammed wants to get in touch with Alex later.*

Mohammed	yaa áliks, kam rágam tilifóon-ak, min fáDHlak?
Alex	dagíigah ... rágam tilifóon-i khámsah, Sifr, tís:ah, síttah, thaláathah, wáaHid.
Mohammed	shúkran, yaa áliks.
Alex	áfwan. wa rágam tilifóon-ak ínta?
Mohammed	rágam tilifóon-i khámsah, ithnáin, wáaHid, sáb:ah, Sifr, thamáanyah.
Alex	shwáyya, shwáyya! márrah tháaniyah, min fáDHlak!
Mohammed	zain. khámsah ... ithnáin ... wáaHid ... sáb:ah ... Sifr ... thamáanyah.
Alex	shúkran, yaa muHámmad.
Mohammed	:áfwan.

> **RÁGAM TILIFÓON-AK ÍNTA YOUR PHONE NUMBER**
> Although it is clear from the suffix **-ak** that the speaker is saying *your phone number*, the added **ínta** emphasizes *your*.

> **TIP**
> **dagíigah** *a minute/moment, hold on*

1 **Find the phrases Alex and Mohammed use for the following:**
   a What's your phone number?
   b My phone number is ...

2 **Are these statements true (T) or false (F)?**
   a Alex asks for Mohammed's phone number.
   b Alex's phone number is 509631.
   c Mohammed's number is 521408.

> **TIP**
> Phone numbers in spoken Arabic are given in a straight series of digits, e.g. 123 456 – just like English.

PRACTICE 2

1 **Rearrange the following numbers in ascending order.**

a síttah	**d** ithnáin
b thaláathah	**e** wáaHid
c khámsah	**f** árba:ah

2 02.09 **Listen to some of these Arabic numbers being read out in random order. Which numbers do you hear?**

   9   2   6   4   3   10   0   1   7   5

3 02.10 **Listen to these words then say them out loud after the speakers. Note the difference in sound between the similar letters, such as S and s, T and t.**

a Sifr	sáb:ah
b briTáaniya	al-imaráat
c faránsa	miSr
d ayrlánda	min fáDHlak

> **PRONUNCIATION TIP**
> Some Arabic words have capital letters in their transliteration. Why? These are different letters from non-capitalized ones. When you pronounce these, hollow your tongue down in your mouth to get the right sound.

4 **Do you remember what the words in exercise 3 mean? Say what they are in English.**

5 02.11 **Listen to the speakers, then note what nationality each person is.**

a _____	**d** _____
b _____	**e** _____
c _____	**f** _____

6 02.12 **Listen to what each person says about themselves and match them with their nationality.**

1 ísm-i saif wa ána min :umaan
2 ísm-i fáadiya, ána yamaníyyah
3 ána nuur wa ána min al-imaaráat
4 ísm-i sáwsan. ána sa:uudiyah (add stress on last syllable)
5 ána ísm-i Hamdáan, wa ána min al-iráaq
6 ísm-i muHámmad. ána gátari

a	Yemen	**d**	Qatar
b	Saudi Arabia	**e**	Emirates
c	Iraq	**f**	Oman

Go further

READING ARABIC

Originally, the ancient Arabic language was written with far fewer letters, many of which had several different pronunciations. To prevent confusion, dots were added to these letters to distinguish between the various pronunciations. In Modern Arabic, the 'dot system' uses the following combinations:

▶ one, two or three dots above the letter
▶ one or two (but not three) dots below the letter.

Many letters have no dots at all.

In this unit you will learn five letters which form the largest group: **b** (**baa'**), **t** (**taa'**), **th** (**thaa'**), **n** (**nuun**) and **y** (**yaa'**). They are almost identical, apart from the number and placement of the dots and the variations in the final and separate forms of two of them: **n** and **y**. All are small in height, and all join both preceding and following letters.

end of a word	middle of a word	start of a word	on its own
كتب **kútub** *books*	سبعة **sáb:ah** *seven*	بحر **báHar** *sea*	ب **baa'**
الكويت **al-kuwáit** *Kuwait*	كتاب **kitáab** *book*	تسعة **tísa:ah** *nine*	ت **taa'**
ثالث **tháalith** *third*	كثير **kathíir** *much*	ثلاثة **thaláathah** *three*	ث **thaa'**
من **min** *from*	بنك **bank** *bank*	نور **nuur** *light*	ن **nuun**
عربي **:árabi** *Arab/Arabic*	جنسية **jinsíyyah** *nationality*	يد **yad** *hand*	ي **yaa'**

1 Match each Arabic letter to its sound.

a ي   **1** nuun
b ت   **2** thaa'
c ن   **3** yaa'
d ث   **4** baa'
e ب   **5** taa'

2 Look at the Arabic words in the table below and match them to their transliteration.

 TIP
In each word, look for the letters you have learned in the first two units, and use the alphabet chart in the Introduction to the Arabic language if you need more help.

	Arabic		Transliteration
a	أنا	1	**lándan**
b	لندن	2	**min**
c	دبي	3	**al-baHráin**
d	من	4	**ána**
e	البحرين	5	**dubáy**

Test yourself

1 **Say these nationalities in Arabic:**
  a English (m)
  b French (f)
  c Qatari (m)
  d Kuwaiti (f)

  e Scottish (m)
  f Bahraini (f)
  g Indian (m)
  h Chinese (f)

2 **Say these numbers in Arabic:**
  a 7
  b 3
  c 9
  d 1

  e 6
  f 2
  g 5
  h 10

3 **How do you say these phone numbers in Arabic?**
  a 055 284 3134
  b 06 183 7499
  c 04 751 6281

SELF CHECK

I CAN . . .

○	... state my nationality.
○	... say what languages I speak.
○	... count from 0 to 10 in Arabic.
○	... ask for and give phone numbers.
○	... ask for someone on the phone.

3

In this unit you will learn how to:
- » say where you live.
- » talk about people's occupations.
- » talk about your family.
- » talk about more than one person.

al-:áa'ilah

My progress tracker

DAY / DATE

Getting to know Arabic speakers

People in the Arab world are famous for their hospitality. Although some Gulf cities such as Dubai can seem to be dominated by expatriates, away from big cities you will not find it difficult to meet local people. Getting to know them may involve an invitation to drink **gáhwah** (*coffee*), eat dates and meet the extended family. This could include **al-wáalid** or **al-ab** (*the father*), **al-wáalidah** or **al-umm** (*the mother*) and **al-awláad** (*the children*), but perhaps also **al-akh** (*the brother*) or **al-ukht** (*the sister*).

People will casually ask personal questions such as **aish ti-shtághal?** (*What do you do for a living?*), or **kam wálad :índ-ak?** to a man or **kam wálad :índ-ich?** to a woman (*How many children* (lit. *child*) *do you have?*). If you arrive alone, a common question is **wain al-awláad?** (*Where are the children?*) But do not take offence at this. Sharing information about each other's work and families is part of getting to know people and of eventually becoming **aSdigáa'** (*friends*), a concept taken very seriously in Arab society.

You may be offered **gáhwah** or **shaay** to drink. What do these words mean?

Vocabulary builder

OCCUPATIONS

03.01 Listen to these occupations and say them out loud, trying to imitate the speakers' pronunciation.

al-mihan	*occupations*
Tabíib	*doctor (male)*
Tabíibah	*doctor (female)*
muhándis	*engineer (male)*
muhándisah	*engineer (female)*
mumárriDH	*nurse (male)*
mumárriDHah	*nurse (female)*
mudárris	*teacher (male)*
mudárrisah	*teacher (female)*
Táalib	*student (male)*
Táalibah	*student (female)*
mudíir sháarikah	*company director (male)*
mudíirat sháarikah	*company director (female)*

> **TIP**
> Words for occupations have different masculine and feminine forms, with an **-ah** sound added to form the feminine.

FAMILY MEMBERS

03.02 First add the missing words, then listen and try to imitate the speakers.

al-:áa'ilah	*the family*
zooj	*husband*
zóojah	*wife*
wálad (awláad)	*boy/son (boys/sons – pl)*
	(can also mean children)
bint (banáat)	*girl/daughter (_____/_____)*
ab *or* wáalid	*father*
umm *or* wáalidah	*mother*
akh (ikhwáan)	*brother (brothers)*
ukht (akhawáat)	*sister (_____)*

> **TIP**
> In Arabic, you tend to call step/half-siblings just 'brother' or 'sister' (possibly adding, 'from a different mother/father'); the technical term for a step-brother translates as 'a brother who isn't fully connected/related,' which sounds like you have fallen out!

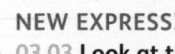

NEW EXPRESSIONS

03.03 Look at these words and expressions, then listen and practice by imitating the pronunciation of the speakers.

wain tí-skun?	*Where do you live?* (to a man)	a-shtághal fii ...	*I (_____) in ...*
wain tí-skun-íin?	*Where do you live?* (to a woman)	mádrasah	*a school*
		mustáshfa	*a hospital*
al-Hiin	*now*	bank	*a bank*
á-skun fii ...	*I live in ...*	sháarikah	*a company*
aish ti-shtághal?	*What do you do* (lit. work)? (to a man)	máktab	*an office*
		kabíir	*big* (m)
aish ti-shtaghal-íin?	*What do you do* (lit. work)? (to a woman)	kabíirah	*big* (f)
		láakin	*but*
ána mumárriDH	*I'm a nurse* (male)		
ána mumárriDHah	*I'm a nurse* (female)		
maa a-shtághal	*I don't work*		

> **TIP**
>
> **mubramij kombuter**   *computer programmer* (male)
> **mubarmijat kombuter**   *computer programmer* (female)
> **ána muhándisah**   *I'm an engineer* (female)
> **ána muhándis**   *I'm an engineer* (male)
> **sháarikah birmujeyat**   *a software company*
> **istudiu tasmiim jirafiki**   *a graphic design studio*

al-Hiin door-ak! *Now your turn!*

Cofi is a teacher. How would he say in Arabic where he works?

Hiwáar 1 *Conversation 1*

03.04 *Rahma and Sally are talking about where they live, and what they and their husbands do for a living. Listen while you follow the text, then answer the questions.*

1 Where does Sally live? Does she work?

Rahma	wain ti-skun-íin al-Hiin ya sáali?
Sally	á-skun fii dubáy. wa íntu wain ti-skun-úun?
Rahma	ná-skun fii másqaT láakin níHna min Suur.

Sally	w ínti aish ti-shtaghal-íin?
Rahma	ána mumárriDHah - a-shtághal fii mustáshfa. w ínti?
Sally	ána maa a-shtághal al-Hiin láakin zóoj-i muhándis, yi-shtághal fii sháarikah kabíirah fii ábu DHábi. wa zooj-ich, aish yi-shtághal?
Rahma	yi-shtághal al-Hiin fii bank.
Sally	maa shaa' Alláah.

2 Read the text again, then answer the questions.

   a What does Rahma do for a living?

   b Where does Sally's husband work?

   c Where does Rahma's husband work?

3 What are these phrases in Arabic? Say your answers out loud.

   a Where do you (f) live now?   **d** What do you (f) do?

   b We live in Muscat.   **e** I'm a computer programmer.

   c ... but we are from Sur.   **f** I don't work.

Language discovery

1 What Arabic word is used in the conversation for *we* and *you* (plural)?

2 What do these three forms of the verb *to work* mean?

   Example: a *I work*

   a a-shtághal   **b** ti-shtaghal-íin   **c** yi-shtághal

1 PLURAL PRONOUNS

In Arabic the pronouns used for *we*, *you* (pl) and *they* are the same, whether you are talking about males or females.

níHna	*we*
íntu	*you*
húmma	*they*

2 PRESENT TENSE VERBS

To form the present tense in Arabic you need a present stem (the 'core' of the verb), a prefix (letters before the stem) and in some cases a suffix (letters after the stem). In Arabic, the present stem of the verb *to live* is **skun**.

Arabic – singular	English	Arabic – plural	English
(ána) á-skun	I live	(níHna) ná-skun	we live
(ínta) tí-skun	you (m) live	(íntu) ti-skun-úun	you (m/f) live
(ínti) ti-skun-íin	you (f) live		
(húwwa) yí-skun	he lives	(húmma) yi-skun-úun	they (m/f) live
(híyya) tí-skun	she lives		

Notes

1 Pronouns (**ána, ínta, ínti**, etc.) are not always used with verbs as the verb prefix and in some cases suffix tells us who or what the subject is. The verb forms for you (m) and she are identical, but it is the context that tells us who is the subject of the verb.

2 Many people from the Gulf alter or omit the vowel of the prefixes **yi-** and **ti-**, so you may hear **yu-, tu-, ya-, ta-** or even **y-, t-**.

3 Some dialects omit the final **-n** in the endings **-íin** and **-úun**.

al-Hiin door-ak! *Now your turn!*

Complete the verb work using the correct pronouns, prefixes, suffixes and English translations.

Arabic – singular	English	Arabic – plural	English
(ána) _____ -shtághal	_____ work	_____ na-shtághal	we work
(ínta) _____ -shtaghal	you (m) work	(íntu) ti-shtághal-úun	_____ (m/f, pl) work
(ínti) ti-shtághal _____	you (f) work		
(húwwa) _____ -shtághal	he works	(húmma) _____ -shtaghal-úun	they (m/f) work
(híyya) ti-shtághal	_____ works		

In Arabic there is no word for the indefinite article, i.e. *a* or *an*. Instead, just use the noun on its own. For example:

ána Tabíib.   *I (am) (a) doctor (m).*
a-shtághal fii mustáshfa.   *I work in (a) hospital.*

al-Hiin door-ak! *Now your turn!*

How would you say the following sentence? *He works in a company.*

PRACTICE 1

1 **Choose the correct pronoun to complete each sentence.**

   a níHna/húmma yi-skun-úun fii :ajmáan.

   b ínti/ínta ti-skun-íin wain?

   c níHna/ána a-shtághal fii gáTar al-Hiin.
   d íntu/níHna ti-shtaghal-úun wain?

2 **Choose the correct form of the verb *to work* to complete each sentence.**
   a húwwa yi-shtághal/ti-shtághal fii bank.
   b híyya ti-shtaghal-íin/ti-shtághal fii mustáshfa.
   c ána a-shtághal/yi-shtághal fii sháarikah kabíirah.
   d húmma na-shtághal/yi-shtaghal-úun fii dubáy.

3 **Choose the correct word for each person's job, depending on whether the subject is masculine or feminine.**
   a híyya mudárris/mudárrisah. (*She (is a) teacher.*)
   b húwwa Tabíibah/Tabíib. (*He (is a) doctor.*)
   c sáalim (m) mikáaniki/mikaanikíyyah. (*He (is a) mechanic.*)
   d fáaTimah (f) muhándisah/muhándis. (*She (is an) engineer.*)

4 **Rearrange the order of the Arabic words below so that the sentence matches its English translation.**

   sháarikah a-shtághal wa muhándis ána fii

   I am an engineer and I work in a company.

5 **Answer these questions about yourself.**
   a wain tí-skun/ti-skun-íin? (*Where do you live?*)
   b aish ti-shtághal/ti-shtaghal-íiin? (*What do you do?*)
   c wain ti-shtághal/ti-shtaghal-íin? (*Where do you work?*)

 6 **Read what these people say about their work, then decide whether the person speaking is male (m) or female (f).**
   a ána muhándisah, ashtághal fii sháarikah.
   b ashtághal fii mádrasah, ána mudárris.
   c ána Tabíib, a-shtághal fii mustáshfa.
   d ána maa a-shtághal, ána Táalibah.
   e ána mudíirat sháarikah.
   f ána mumárriDH, ashtághal fii mustáshfa.

7 **Are these people talking about one person (singular) or more than one person (plural)?**
   a málik yí-skun fi l-baHráin.
   b sáarah wa Táariq yi-skun-úun fii bait kabíir.
   c ti-skun-úun fi l-dooHah?
   d jain tí-skun fi l-kuwáit.

Listen and understand

 1 03.05 **What do these people do for a living? Careful – there are some extra jobs you won't need!**

a :áli
b máriyam
c fáaris
d básma
e jamáal
f híbah
g mubramij kombuter

computer programmer
influencer   student
company director   engineer
nurse   teacher   doctor
mechanic   bank manager

2 03.06 **Add the missing word to complete the English translation.**

a I am a _____.
b He works in a _____.
c My parents _____ in Bahrain.
d Do you _____ in Dubai?
e Where does he _____?
f She doesn't _____ in Al-Ain.

Hiwáar 2 *Conversation 2*

03.07 *First listen to Fatima and Sally talk about their families, then answer the questions.*

1 How many children does Sally have? What are their ages?

Fatima	:índ-ich awláad ya sáali?
Sally	áywa, :índi wálad wa bint.
Fatima	(*laughing*) bass?
Sally	(*laughing with her*) áywa, w ínti?
Fatima	níHna :índ-na síttah, thaláthah awláad wa thaláth banáat.
Sally	maa shaa' Alláah!
Fatima	al-wálad kam :úmr-uh?
Sally	mm, al-wálad :úmr-uh tís:a wa l-bint :úmr-ha khámas sanawáat.

kam wálad :índ-ich?	How many children do you (f) have? (can also mean How many boys/sons do you have?)
(ána) :índ-i	I have
(níHna) :índ-na	we have
maa sháa' Alláah	God has willed it (a term of appreciation, gratitude and amazement)
al-awláad kam :úmr-hum?	How old are your children?
:úmr-uh khámas sanawáat.	He is five years old.
:úmr-ha thamáan sanawáat.	She is eight years old.

>
> **maa sháa' Alláah** is often used to express joy, appreciation or gratitude and literally means *God has willed it*. Often used to ward off jealousy or misfortune, it can be seen on cars, shop windows and even street signs as a reminder that all accomplishments are achieved by the will of God, including the journey home.

 2 03.07 **Listen to the conversation again, then answer these questions.**

    a How many children does Sally have?

    b How many daughters does Fatima have?

    c How old is Sally's daughter?

 3 **Can you say the Arabic for the following?**

    a Do you (f) have any children?

    b Is that all?!

    c We have six.

Language discovery

1 **What is the Arabic word for *three girls/daughters*?**

2 **If :úmr-i means *my age*, to what do the endings on the words :úmr-uh and :úmr-ha in the conversation refer?**

1 PLURALS

Arabic plurals are often irregular so the best approach is to learn the plural together with the singular of a noun.

wálad (boy/son)	**awláad** (boys/sons)
sánah (year)	**sanawáat** (years)

2 POSSESSIVE SUFFIXES

You have already learned the possessive suffix endings for *my* and *your* (sing.) Here are the endings for *his, her, our, your* (pl) and *their*.

Arabic possessive suffix	English possessive pronoun
-uh	*his*
-ha	*her*
-na	*our*
-kum	*your* (m/f, pl)
-hum	*their* (m/f)

:úmr-**uh** sitt sanawáat	*he is six years old* (lit. *life-his six years*)
bint-**ha** ísm-**ha** jamíilah	*her daughter is called Jamila* (lit. *daughter-her name-her Jamila*)

> **SITT OR SITTAH?**
> Arabic has both feminine and masculine forms of numbers, e.g. **sitt** (m) and **sittah** (f), and there are special rules as to when to use which. For further details, see *Complete Spoken Arabic* or *Complete Arabic*.

PRACTICE 2

1 **Add the correct plural form of these words. Refer to the Vocabulary builder at the start of the unit if you need help.**
   a bint (*girl*) _____ **b** akh (*brother*) _____ **c** ukht (*sister*) _____

2 **Complete each sentence by adding the correct word in each space.**
   a :índ-i thaláathah _____ (*boys*) wa thaláth _____ (*girls*).
   b bínt-i :úmr-ha khámas _____ (*years (old)*).
   c :índ-i árba: _____ (*sisters*).

3 **Choose the correct possessive suffix for the following:**
   a bínt-i :úmr(-uh/-ha) áab:a sanawáat.
   b ákh-i úmr(-uh/-ha) :sitt sanawáat.
   c al-awláad :úmr(-na/-hum) thaláth wa thamáan sanawáat.

   Now translate each sentence into English.

Go further

READING ARABIC

The group of letters **j** (**jiim**), **H** (**Haa'**) and **kh** (**khaa'**) all have the same basic shape and are distinguished only by dots. Remember to refer to the Pronunciation guide when practicing the sound of these letters.

j or ج has a dot below the basic shape.

H or ح has no dot at all.

kh or خ has a dot above the basic shape.

In handwriting, including calligraphy on street shops and signs, the joining strokes from the previous letters are often looped over the top like this:

end of a word	middle of a word	start of a word	alone
الخليج **al-khalíij** *the Gulf*	عجمان **:ajmáan** *Ajman (an Emirate)*	جدة **jáddah** *grandmother*	ج **jiim**
صالح **SáaliH** *Salih (a male's name)*	البحرين **al-baHráin** *Bahrain (a country)*	حمد **Hámad** *Hamad (a male's name)*	ح **Haa'**
شيخ **shaikh** *sheikh (ruler)*	أخت **ukht** *sister*	خلود *khuluud (a female's name)*	خ **khaa'**

> **TIP**
> The second letter in this group, **H**, is very common in the numerous personal names which derive from the root **H-m-d** meaning *praise*, e.g. **muHámmad**, **Hámad**, **maHmúud** and **áHmad**.

Match the Arabic writing to its correct transliteration in Arabic. For help, look out for the letters in their different positions (beginning, middle and end of a word).

	Arabic		Transliteration
a	جنوب	1	Hámad (name)
b	زوجة	2	al-baHráin (Bahrain)
c	حمد	3	khaTT (script)
d	أخت	4	akh (brother)
e	الخليج	5	janúub (south)
f	أخ	6	zóojah (wife)
g	البحرين	7	al-khalíij (the Gulf)
h	خط	8	ukht (sister)

Test yourself

Read the message Fatima writes to introduce herself and her family, then answer the question.

1 Can you guess the meaning of rábbat al-bait?

✉ — ⤢ ✕

ána ísm-i fáaTimah wa á-skun fii nizwa fii :umáan. :úmr-i :ishríin sánah. abú-i ísm-uh kháalid. húwwa muhándis wa yi-shtághal fii shárikah kabíirah fii nízwa. úmm-i maa ti-shtághal, híyya rábbat al-bait. :índi thaláathah ikhwáan wa húmma yi-shtaghal-úun fii másqaT.

✈ 📎 ☺

> **TIP**
> **bait** house
> **:ashríin** twenty
> **abú-i** my father

2 Answer these questions to check your understanding.

a Where does Fatima live?

b How old is she?

c What does Fatima's father do?

d How many brothers does Fatima have?

3 Choose the correct word to complete each sentence.

a ána :úmr-i/:úmr-uh thalaathíin sánah.

b ínti ti-shtághal/ti-shtaghal-íin wain?

c al-wálad kam :úmr-uh/:úmr-ha?

d bint-i yí-skun/tí-skun fii jáddah.

e abú-i maa yi-shtághal/ti-shtághal al-Hiin.

TIP
thalaathíin *thirty*

4 Use what you have learned in this unit to answer these questions about yourself. Say your answers out loud.

a wain tí-skun/ti-skun-íin?

b aish ti-shtághal/ti-shtaghal-íin?

c :índ-ak/:índ-ich awláad/ikhwáan/akhawáat?

SELF CHECK

I CAN . . .
... say where I live.
... talk about people's occupations.
... talk about my family.
... talk about more than one person.

R1 Review: Units 1–3

1 You have just met Mohammed at the conference banquet at 7 p.m. Greet him out loud with the correct Arabic phrase.

  a SabáaH al-khair.
  b má: as-saláamah.
  c masáa' al-khair.
  d al-Hámdu li-l-láah bi-kháir.

2 Match the Arabic to the English, saying the Arabic out loud.

  a ána ísm-i ...
  b kaif Háal-ak?
  c al-Hámdu li-l-láah bi-kháir.
  d ána min lándan.
  e ta-takállam inglíizi?
  f aish ti-shtághal?
  g má:a as-saláamah.

  1 I'm fine, thanks.
  2 What do you do?
  3 I'm from London.
  4 Goodbye.
  5 My name is ...
  6 Do you speak English?
  7 How are you?

3 There are two words for *you* (singular) in Arabic – **ínta** or **ínti**. Which would you use for the following people?

  a your sister
  b your female boss
  c your friend's brother
  d the male receptionist

4 Match the English to the correct possessive endings in Arabic.

  a my
  b your (m)
  c your (f)
  d his
  e her

  1 -ak
  2 -ha
  3 -i
  4 -ich/-ish/-ik
  5 -uh

5 You want to know a little more about Mohammed. Match each question to its correct translation, then say the Arabic out loud.

  a Where do you come from?
  b Where do you live?
  c What do you do?
  d Do you speak English?
  e Do you have children?

  1 ta-takállam inglíizi?
  2 aish ti-shtághal?
  3 :ind-ak awláad?
  4 wain tí-skun?
  5 ínta min wain?

6 **Give the feminine form for each of these words.**

   a ána inglíiz-i   _____
   b ána gáTar-i   _____
   c ána Tabíib   _____
   d ána mudárris   _____
   e ána amríik-i   _____

7 **What does each phrase in the previous exercise mean in English?**

8 **Match the number words in transliterated Arabic to the correct English and Arabic numerals.**

a	ithnáin	1	٥
b	:áshara	7	٨
c	khámsah	3	١
d	thaláathah	8	٢
e	sáb:ah	2	١٠
f	wáaHid	5	٣
g	thamáanyah	10	٧

9 **You have just met an Arabic speaker who asks you the following questions. Answer each question out loud in Arabic, giving information about yourself. Try to speak with good pronunciation!**

   a aish ísm-ak/ísm-ich?
   b ínta/ínti min wain?
   c wain tí-skun/ti-skun-íin?
   d ta-takállam :árabi?
   e kam rágam tilifóon-ak?
   f wain ti-shtághal/ti-shtaghal-íin al-Hiin?
   g :índ-ak/:índ-ich awláad?

10 **This sign says 'Now open'. Which Arabic word means maftúuH (_open_)?**

   a the top word
   b the bottom word

11 The Arabic word for *post* is **baríid** and the Arabic for *office* is **máktab**.

　a Which of the Arabic words in the sign says **baríid**: the first or the second?

　b Which word has **al** (*the*) in front of it, **baríid** or **máktab**?

Try to identify the letters you have learned in Units 1 to 3.

4

In this unit you will learn how to:
» ask for and tell the time.
» ask when places open or close.
» talk about days of the week.
» talk about different times of day.

kam as-sáa:ah?

My progress tracker

DAY / DATE

Hours of the day

The working day in the Gulf starts between **as-sáa:ah sába:ah** (*seven o'clock*) and **as-sáa:ah thamáanyah** (*eight o'clock*) in the morning and for many government workers ends between one and two **bá:d aDH-Dhuhr** (*in the afternoon*). Were you to visit a ministry or other government department at 3 p.m., you would probably find it **magfúul** (*closed*) for the day, but the **suug** (*market*) and smaller businesses open again later in the afternoon when temperatures are cooler. This is when families go shopping together, and you will often see groups of women haggling with the **khayyáaT** (*tailor*) over the price and completion date of a custom-made dress, people buying their food for the week, and others just enjoying the chance to get out for a walk.

Visitors to the region are often surprised to learn that the weekend in most Gulf countries falls on **yoom al-júma:ah** (*Friday*) and **yoom as-sabt** (*Saturday*). **al-júma:ah** is the Muslim day of prayer and in most parts of the Gulf offices and businesses are closed all day on Friday and Saturday. However, for the **suug**, the mall and other smaller shops, it is a seven-day week wherever you are.

> **TIP**
> The word **yoom** is often omitted, especially with **al-júma:ah**.

If **yoom ath-thaláathah** (*Tuesday*) means *the third day*, can you work out which numbers these days of the week correspond to?
al-ithnáin, al-árba:ah, al-khamíis

Vocabulary builder

TIMES OF THE DAY

04.01 Fill the gap, then listen and try to imitate the pronunciation of the speakers.

aS-Súb(a)H	*(the) morning*
aDH-DHúh(u)r	*noon*
bá:d aDH-Dhúh(u)r	*afternoon* (lit. *after the-noon*)
al-mása	*(the) evening*
al-lail	*(the) night*
as-sáa:ah sáb:ah aS-Súb(a)H	*7 a.m.*
as-sáa:ah tís:ah fi l-lail	*9 _____*

NEW EXPRESSIONS

04.02 Fill the gap, then listen and try to imitate the pronunciation of the speakers.

kam as-sáa:ah?	*What time is it?*
as-sáa:ah thaláathah.	*It's _____ o'clock.*
bi DH-DHabt	*exactly*
wa nuSS	*half past*
fiih maT:am hína fi l-fúndug (funduq)?	*Is there a restaurant here in the hotel?*
fiih ...	*There is ...*
máT:am	*(a) restaurant*
másbaH	*(a) pool*
yí-ftaH	*it opens* (m)
tí-ftaH	*it opens* (f)
yi-bánnid	*it closes* (m)
ti-bánnid	*it closes* (f)
yí-ftaH as-sáa:ah kam?	*What time does it* (m) *_____?*
tí-ftaH as-sáa:ah kam?	*What time does it* (f) *_____?*
fi l-lail	*in the evening*
maftúuH	*open* (m)
maftúuHah	*open* (f)
magfúul (maqfúul)	*closed* (m)
magfúulah (maqfúulah)	*_____* (f)

tagríiban (taqríiban)	*approximately, around*
aw	*or*
ashkúr-ak	*(I) thank you* (to a man)
ashkúr-_____	*(I) thank you* (to a woman)
áhlan wa sáhlan	*hello, also (you're) welcome*

> **TIP**
> You may hear the local words **mbánnad** (*closed*) and **mbáTTal** (*open*) but as these can't be used in all contexts, it's best to stick to **magfúul** and **maftúuH**.

Hiwáar 1 *Conversation 1*

04.03 *Peter has just arrived at a hotel in Muscat after a night flight from London. He asks the receptionist about the local time as his phone has not updated automatically. First listen, then answer the question.*

1 What is the time difference between London and Muscat?

Peter	yaa akhú-i, kam as-sáa:ah?
káatib	al-Hiin as-sáa:ah sáb:ah.
Peter	as-sáa:ah sáb:ah bi DH-DHábt?
káatib	ná:am, bi DH-DHábt.
Peter	shúkran.
káatib	:áfwan.
Peter	fiih máT:am híni fi l-fúndug?
káatib	ná:am, fiih. ... láakin húwwa magfúul al-Hiin.
Peter	as-sáa:ah kam yí-ftaH?
káatib	yí-ftaH as-sáa:ah sáb:ah wa nuSS, yá:ani ... ba:d nuSS sáa:ah.
Peter	ashkúr-ak.
káatib	áhlan wa sáhlan.

> **TIP**
> The conversation above uses the term:
> **káatib**   *receptionist* (m)
> However in the Gulf, you are more likely to hear the term **muwáDHaf istiqbáal** instead.
> **híni**   *variation of* **hína** (*here*)

> **TIP**
> **akhú-i**, literally meaning *my brother*, is a friendly term often used to address a man, even if you don't know him. Similarly, you can use the term **úkht-i**, *my sister*, for a woman.

04.04 *Peter goes on to ask about the pool.*

Peter	wa fiih másbaH?
káatib	áiwa fiih.
Peter	as-sáa:ah kam yi-bánnid fi l-lail?
káatib	yá:ani … as-sáa:ah síttah aw sába:ah tagríiban.
Peter	shúkran.
káatib	:áfwan.

 TIP

The term **yá:ani** has various meanings such as *well, hmm, kind of, sort of*. You will hear it a lot and in order to sound really authentic you should start using it right away!

2 **When does the restaurant open?**

3 **How long must Peter wait before he can get something to eat at the restaurant?**

4 **What two things does he ask about the pool?**

Language discovery

1 **Find the phrase which means *seven o'clock*.**

2 **Find the phrase which means *It is closed now*.**

TELLING THE TIME

 04.05 To say *o'clock* in Arabic, just say **as-sáa:ah** plus a number. It can mean both *it is … o'clock* and *at … o'clock*.

kam as-sáa:ah?	*What time is it?*
as-sáa:ah wáaH(i)dah	*one o'clock*
as-sáa:ah thintáin	*two o'clock*
as-sáa:ah thaláathah	*three o'clock*
as-sáa:ah árba:ah	*four o'clock*
as-sáa:ah khámsah	*five o'clock*
as-sáa:ah síttah	*six o'clock*
as-sáa:ah sába:ah	*seven o'clock*
as-sáa:ah thamáanyah	*eight o'clock*
as-sáa:ah tís:ah	*nine o'clock*
as-sáa:ah :ásharah	*ten o'clock*
as-sáa:ah (iHdá:shar)	*eleven o'clock*

as-sáa:ah (ithná:shar)	twelve o'clock
wa khams	five past
wa rúba:	quarter past
wa thilth	twenty past (lit. *and a third (of an hour)*)
wa nuSS	half past
ílla thilth	twenty to (lit. *less a third (of an hour)*)
ílla rubu:	a quarter to (lit. *less a quarter*)
ílla khams	five to (lit. *less five*)

> **TIP**
>
> In English you say *past*, but in Arabic you say **wa** (*and* or *plus*):
> **as-sáa:ah wáaHdah wa rubu:** lit. *the hour is one plus a quarter (quarter past one)*

Twenty-five past and *twenty-five to* the hour are expressed in Arabic as *the hour plus a half minus five*, and *the hour plus a half plus five*, respectively.

as-sáa:ah khámsah wa-nuSS ílla khams   *twenty-five past five*

as-sáa:ah khámsah wa-nuSS wa khams   *twenty-five to six*

GENDER OF NOUNS

In Arabic, nouns are either masculine or feminine in gender. So when you want to ask when somewhere is open or closed, you need to know if the place is masculine or feminine so that you can use the correct verb form or adjective. In English we would say *it* but in Arabic you use **húwwa** (*he*) and **híyya** (*she*) for non-human nouns.

húwwa magfúul   lit. *he is closed*

híyya magfúulah   lit. *she is closed*

Equally, you must use either the masculine or feminine verb form according to the gender of the noun.

al-máT:am yí-ftaH   *the restaurant opens*
   (**máT:am** is masculine)

aS-Saydalíyyah tí-ftaH   *the pharmacy opens*
   (**Saydalíyyah** is feminine)

As a general rule, most nouns ending in **-ah** are feminine but there are exceptions such as **umm** (*mother*) and **bint** (*girl*), which are both feminine.

1 **Match the correct time to each statement.**

   a as-sáa:ah árba:ah wa rubu: 3:45/4:15
   b as-sáa:ah khámsah ílla thilth   4:40/5:20
   c as-sáa:ah thamáanyah wa nuSS   8:30/9:30
   d as-sáa:ah iHdá:shar wa khams   10:55/11:05
   e as-sáa:ah thintáin wa nuSS ílla khams 2:25/2:35

2 **First ask what the time is, then say the time shown on each clock face.**

3 **Select the correct word for *open* and *closed* according to the gender of each noun as given.**

   a as-suug (m)   maftúH/maftúHah
   b as-síinima (f)   maftúH/maftúHah
   c al-bank (m)   magfúul/magfúulah
   d al-baríid (m)   maftúH/maftúHah
   e al-mustáshfa (f)   magfúul/magfúulah

> **TIP**
>
> | (Maktab) baríid | *post office* |
> | shárikat al-baríid as-saríi:ah | *courier company* |
> | shárikah at-tawSiil | *delivery company* |
>
> Post offices are still common in Arab countries, especially in towns and rural areas, but they are decreasing in cities where they are being replaced by couriers like UPS and DHL.

Listen and understand

1 04.06 Listen, then select the correct time for each statement.

- **a** 7:00/8:00/9:00
- **b** 9:30/11:30/3:30
- **c** 4:05/4:25/4:35
- **d** 2:15/3:15/3:45
- **e** 6:50/7:10/7:50
- **f** 11:55/12:05/12:55

2 04.06 Listen again and repeat the times. Take care to pronounce the **:ain** in **sáa:ah** correctly.

3 Now answer the question giving the current time.

kam as-sáa:ah al-Hiin?

Hiwáar 2 *Conversation 2*

04.07 *Anya is spending Friday afternoon at the shopping mall. At the information desk she asks for some opening and closing times. First listen, then answer the question.*

1 What is the first place Anya asks about?

Anya	masáa' al khair.
káatib	masáa' an-nuur.
Anya	fiih baríid fi l-mool?
káatib	aywa fiih, garíib min as-síinima.
Anya	húwwa maftúuH al-Hiin?
káatib	laa, húwwa magfúul yoom al-júma:ah.
Anya	Táb:an! aS-Saydalíyyah magfúulah ba:d?
káatib	laa, híyya maftúHah.
Anya	as-sáa:ah kam ti-bánnid?
káatib	ti-bánnid as-sáa:ah khámsah.
Anya	w as-síinima, as-sáa:ah kam tí-ftaH fi l-lail?
káatib	as-síinima maftúHah Tool al-yoom kull yoom! ti-bánnid as-sáa:ah ithná:shar fi l-lail.
Anya	shúkran jazíilan.
káatib	:áfwan.

TIP

ba:d	*also, too* (also *still* and *after* depending on context)
Tool al-yoom	*all day*
kull* yoom	*every day*

***kull** is often pronounced **kill** in the Gulf.

2 What is the problem with the first place Anya would like to visit?

3 Is the pharmacy open right now?

4 When is the cinema open?

 5 04.07 Listen again and speak the part of Anya. You begin.

Language discovery

ayáam al-usbúu	*Days of the week*
yoom al-áHad	*Sunday*
yoom al-ithnáin	*Monday*
yoom ath-thaláathah	*Tuesday*
yoom al-árba:ah	*Wednesday*
yoom al-khamíis	*Thursday*
yoom al-júma:ah	*Friday*
yoom as-sabt	*Saturday*

1 Can you find the phrase in the conversation that means the following?
It is closed on Friday.

2 As the next day starts from sundown in Islam, sunset on Saturday is the beginning of Sunday. So, if you receive an invitation to a wedding on **láilat al-áHad** (lit. *night of Sunday*), when should you turn up?
   a Sunday evening   b Sunday morning   c Saturday evening

3 What does **ti-bánnid as-sáa:ah ithná:ashar fi l-lail** mean?

Now that you know how to tell the time, and say the days of the week and times of the day, you can begin to make longer sentences, giving more information.

<u>al-bank</u> **yi-ftaH as-sáa:ah kam yoom** <u>al-áHad aSabaaH</u>?

What time does the bank open on Sunday morning?

<u>al-mool</u> **yi-bánnid as-sáa:ah kam yoom** <u>al-khamíis fi l-lail</u>?

What time does the mall close on Thursday evening?

al-Hiin door-ak! *Now your turn!*

Using the examples as a guide, translate these questions into Arabic, changing the underlined words to say the following instead.

   a What time does the <u>pool</u> (m) open on <u>Wednesday morning</u>?

   b What time does the <u>restaurant</u> (m) close on <u>Saturday evening</u>?

PRACTICE 2

1 **When do these places open or close? Say the question then the answer in Arabic, being sure to include the correct time of day.**

Example: a al-bank yí-ftaH as-sáa:ah kam? yí-ftaH as-sáa:ah thamáanyah aSabaaH.

a bank (m) opens?	at 8 a.m.
b mall (m) opens?	at 9 a.m.
c cinema (f) closes?	at 11.30 p.m.
d police station (m) opens?	at 7.15 a.m.
e shop (m) closes?	at 1.30 p.m.

2 **Read these times and write them out in English.**

   a ١١:٣٠   **d** ١٢:١٥

   b ٩:١٠   **e** ١٠:٠٠

   c ٧:٢٥   **f** ٢٣:٠٠

3 **Can you identify the business hours from morning to evening?**

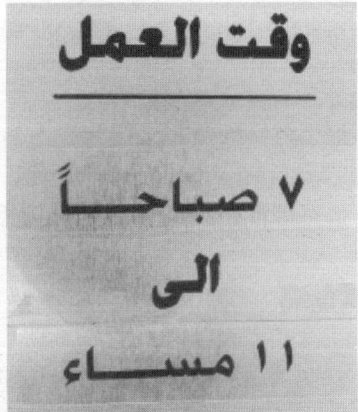

وقت العمل

٧ صباحاً

الى

١١ مساء

Go further

READING ARABIC

The letters **d** د and **dh** ذ are called **daal** and **dhaal**. **daal** and **dhaal** are two of the six letters that don't join onto the letter that follows them, as you can see in the table.

end of a word	middle of a word	start of a word	on its own
ولد **wálad** *boy*	صيدلية **Saydalíyyah** *pharmacy*	دكان **dukkáan** *shop*	د **daal**
خذ **khudh** *take*	هذا **háadha** *this* (m)	ذلك **dháalik** *that*	ذ **dhaal**

1 Find the letter (daal) or (dhaal) in the following table. Do these letters appear at the beginning (B), middle (M) or end (E) of each word?

	Transliteration and meaning	Arabic word	Letter position
a	**awláad** *boys*	أولاد	B M E
b	**dubáy** *Dubai*	دبي	B M E
c	**baghdáad** *Baghdad*	بغداد	B M E
d	**jáddah** *grandmother*	جدة	B M E
e	**háadha** *this* (m)	هذا	B M E
f	**dukkáan** *shop*	دكان	B M E
g	**ad-dóoHah** *Doha*	الدوحة	B M E
h	**al-áHad** *Sunday*	الأحد	B M E

2 Now highlight the letters **daal** and/or **dhaal** in each word.

Test yourself

 1 Say these times in Arabic, including the time of day.

Example: a as-sáa:ah thamáanyah aS-SúbaH

a 8 a.m.   e 9.45 a.m.

b 2.30 p.m.   f 5.15 p.m.

c 6.10 p.m.   g 7.30 a.m.

d 4 p.m.   h 11.20 p.m.

 2 How do you say these days of the week in Arabic?

a Tuesday   d Friday

b Saturday   e Monday

c Thursday   f Sunday

SELF CHECK

I CAN . . .
... ask for and tell the time.
... ask when places open or close.
... talk about the days of the week.
... talk about different times of day.

5

In this unit you will learn how to:

» ask for an item in a shop.
» recognize prices online.
» ask for something different.
» say what colour something is.
» recognize and use numbers 11 to 1 million.
» ask about prices.

bi-kám háadha?

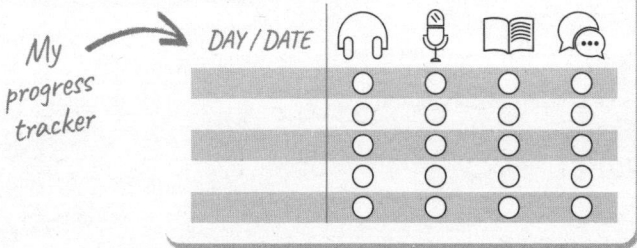

My progress tracker

DAY / DATE

Shopping

Although many purchases are made online, there is still a place for face-to-face shopping in the Gulf, whether you seek top-end designer goods in a modern, air-conditioned **márkaz tijáari** or **mool** (*shopping centre* or *mall*), or prefer to barter for something more traditional in the bustling **suug**, where you will find all sorts of wonderful items. You may be tempted to buy a **mabkharah** or **míjmar** (*incense burner*), some **lubáan** (*frankincense*), or even a **khánjar** (*decorative dagger*). Haggling over prices in the **suug** is fun and a great way to escape the heat of the midday sun. At the glittering **suug adh-dháhab** (*gold market*) you can buy and sell, trading in your **kháaTim gadíim** (*old ring*) or your **silsílah gadíimah** (*old necklace*) for the latest design at today's gold price. Whatever you are shopping for, you will need to know phrases such as **ti-sáwwi takhfíiDH?** (*Will you give me a discount?*) and **bikám áakhir?** (*What's your last price?*)

In a souvenir shop you hear someone ask **al-khánjar bikám?** What does this mean in English?

Vocabulary builder

05.01 Listen, then repeat the words and phrases and try to imitate the speaker's pronunciation.

fi s-suuq (suuq)	*at the market*
míjmar (m), mabkharah	*incense burner*
bakhúur (m)	*spice incense mix*
lubáan (m)	*frankincense*
finjáan (m)	*(coffee) cup*
gamíiS/qamíiS (m)	*shirt*
fustáan (m)	*dress*
bantalóon (m)	*trousers*
kháaTim (m)	*ring*
silsílah (f)	*necklace*
zoolíyyah (f), sijjadah	*carpet*

TIP

sharihat jawaal / SIM bitakah (f) *SIM card*

ADJECTIVES

kabíir/kabíirah	*big* (m/f)
Saghíir/Saghíirah	*small* (m/f)
Tawíil/Tawíilah	*long/tall* (m/f)
gaSíir/gaSíirah	*short* (m/f)
gháali/gháaliyah	*expensive* (m/f)
rakhíiS/rakhíiSah	*cheap* (m/f)
jamíil/jamíilah	*beautiful* (m/f)
jadíid/jadíidah	*new* (m/f)
gadíim/gadíimah (qadíim)	*old* (m/f)

NEW EXPRESSIONS

05.02 Look at these phrases, then listen and practice by imitating the pronunciation of the speakers.

aish tiríid/tirid-íin?	*What do you want?* (to a man/woman)
a-ríid a-shúuf	*I want to look* (lit. *I-want I-look*)
a-ríid a-shtári	*I want to buy …* (lit. *I-want I-buy*)
tfáDHDHal	*here you are* (to a man)
tfáDHDHali	*here you are* (to a woman)
húwwa gadíim?	*Is it (m) old?* (lit. *Is he old?*)
híyya gadíimah?	*Is it (f) old?* (lit. *Is she old?*)

fiih :índ-ak/-ich ...?	*Do you (m/f) have ...?* (lit. *Is there with you ...?*)
tháani/tháaniyah	*another one* (m/f)
ákbar shwáyya	*a little bigger*
Táb:an	*of course*
wáajid, *also* jíddan	*very*

> **PRONUNCIATION TIP**
>
> In some parts of the Gulf the **j** is pronounced like a **y** or a **g**, so **wáajid** becomes **wáayid** or **wáagid**.

Hiwáar 1 *Conversation 1*

05.03 *Ali is at the* **suug** *in Oman, hoping to find something to take home to his family. First listen, then answer the question.*

1 What is the first item Ali looks at?

Ali	as-saláamu :aláikum.
SáaHib ad-dukkáan	w :aláikum as-saláam. aish ti-ríid?
Ali	a-ríid a-shúuf bass.
(*Ali looks around the shop for a while.*)	
Ali	a-ríid a-shtári míjmar.
SáaHib ad-dukkáan	(*hands one to him*) tfáDHDHal.
Ali	(*peering at it*) húwwa gadíim?
SáaHib ad-dukkáan	laa laa, húwwa jadíid. (*hands him another*) háadha wáajid gadíim.
Ali	shúkran. fiih :índ-ak tháani ákbar shwáyya?
SáaHib ad-dukkáan	Táb:an.
(*Ali looks around the shop a little more.*)	
Ali	wa az-zoolíyyah aS-Saghíirah jadíidah?
SáaHib ad-dukkáan	háadhi? áywa, híyya jadíidah.

>
> **TIP**
>
> **SáaHib ad-dukkáan**   *shopkeeper*

>
> **TIP**
>
> The expression **tfáDHDHal** and its feminine form **tfáDHDHali** are used when handing an item to someone, showing them a door or seat, and also when politely asking them to go ahead first or take their turn.

2 Decide if the sentences are true (T) or false (F).
   a The first item Ali looks at is old.
   b He asks if the shopkeeper has a bigger one.
   c He then looks at a carpet.
   d He asks if it is old.

3 Match each phrase to its correct meaning.
   a a-ríid a-shtári   **1** of course
   b háadhi jadíidah   **2** this incense burner
   c Táb:an   **3** very beautiful
   d :índ-ak tháani ákbar?   **4** this (one) is new (f)
   e wáajid jamíilah   **5** Do you have a bigger one?
   f háadha al-míjmar   **6** I want to buy

4 05.03 **Listen again and repeat, taking the part of Ali. You begin.**

Ali	_____
SáaHib ad-dukkáan	w :aláikum as-saláam. aish ti-ríid?
Ali	_____
(*Ali looks around the shop for a while.*)	
Ali	_____
SáaHib ad-dukkáan	(*hands one to him*) tfáDHDHal.
Ali	_____
SáaHib ad-dukkáan	laa laa, húwwa jadíid.
	(*hands him another*) háadha wáajid gadíim.
Ali	_____
SáaHib ad-dukkáan	Táb:an.
(*Ali looks around the shop a little more.*)	
Ali	_____
SáaHib ad-dukkáan	háadhi? áywa, híyya jadíidah.

Language discovery

Find the expressions in the conversation that mean:
   a bigger   **b** I want to look

COMPARATIVE ADJECTIVES

You learned the adjective **kabíir** (*big*) in Unit 3. To say *bigger*, use the comparative form **ákbar**. Here are some adjectives with their comparative forms.

 05.04

kabíir	*big*	**ákbar**	*bigger*
Saghíir	*small*	**áSghar**	*smaller*
Tawíil	*tall, long*	**áTwal**	*taller, longer*
gaSíir	*short*	**ágSar**	*shorter*
gháali	*expensive*	**ághla**	*more expensive*
rakhíiS	*cheap*	**árkhaS**	*cheaper*
jamíil	*beautiful*	**ájmal**	*more beautiful*
zain	*good*	**áHsan**	*better*

> **TIP**
> The comparative form for adjectives is the same for both genders.

> **TIP**
> To ask for something different, use **tháani** (m) or **tháaniyah** (f).
> **:ind-ak tháani ákbar?**   *Do you* (m) *have a bigger one* (m)?
> (lit. *with-you (a) second/bigger (one)?*)

NUMBERS 11–20

١١	11	**iHdá:shar**
١٢	12	**ithná:shar**
١٣	13	**thalaathtá:shar**
١٤	14	**arba:atá:shar**
١٥	15	**khamsatá:shar**
١٦	16	**sittá:shar**
١٧	17	**sab:atá:shar**
١٨	18	**thamantá:shar**
١٩	19	**tis:atá:shar**
٢٠	20	**:ishríin**

PRACTICE 1

1 Match the items to the Arabic.

a

1 míjmar

b

2 gamíiS

c

3 zoolíyyah

d

4 silsílah

e

5 kháaTim

f

6 finjáan

2 Ali needs a few more items. Separate the words, then write out his shopping list in English.

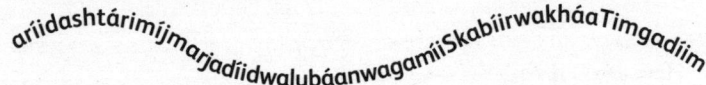

aríidashtárimijmarjadíidwalubáanwagamíiSkabíirwakháaTimgadíim

> **TIP**
> In Arabic, words in lists are linked by **wa** (*and*) rather than by a comma.

 3 Ask the male shopkeeper the following in Arabic.
   a Do you have a smaller one (m)?
   b Do you have a cheaper one (f)?
   c Do you have a taller one (m)?
   d Do you have a shorter one (f)?

4 What do these people want to buy?
   a a-ríid a-shtári bitáaqah SIM.
   b :índ-ak dállah?
   c a-ríid a-shtári bánjari jamíil.
   d a-ríid sáa:ah rakhíisah.
   e :índ-ak gamíiS ákbar?
   f :índ-ak silsílah áTwal?

> **TIP**
>
> | | |
> |---|---|
> | **dállah (f)** | *coffee pot* |
> | **bánjari (m) / iswírah (f)** | *bracelet* |
> | **sáa:ah (f)** | *watch, clock* (also means *hour*) |

TALKING ABOUT PRICES

 05.05 **Listen and repeat, then add the missing English words.**

háadha bikám?	*How much is this?* (m)
háadhi bikám?	*How much is this?* (f)
bi-khámsah riyáal.	*(It costs) _____ riyals.*
gháali/gháaliyah	*expensive*
fiih :índ-ak tháani árkhaS?	*Do you have a _____ one?*
ba:d gháali	*still (too) expensive*
rakhkháS-li shwáyya	*make it a little cheaper (for me)*
maa ágdar	*I can't*
laish?	*Why?*
kill shay gháali	*everything is expensive*
ti-sáwwi takhfíiDH?	*Will you give me a discount?* (lit. *you-make reduction?*)
bi-kám áakhir?	*What's (your) last (price)?*
tamáam	*OK, good*
bíshtari.	*I will buy (it).*
shay tháani?	*Anything else?*

Hiwáar 2 *Conversation 2*

05.06 *Ali opts to buy an incense burner and wants to close the deal. Listen as you read, then answer the question.*

1 How much is the first incense burner?

Ali	háadha l-míjmar al-áHmar bikám?
SáaHib ad-dukkáan	háadha ... bi-khámsah riyáal.
Ali	khámsah riyáal? gháali! fiih :índ-ak tháani árkhaS?
SáaHib ad-dukkáan	háadha bi-thaláathah riyáal.
Ali	laa, laa, laa, ba:d gháali! rakhkháS-li shwáyya!
SáaHib ad-dukkáan	ma ágdar!
Ali	laish?
SáaHib ad-dukkáan	kill shay gháali! (*said smiling*)
Ali	ti-sáwwi takhfíiDH?
SáaHib ad-dukkáan	riyaaláin wa nuSS.
Ali	(*laughs*) bikám áakhir?
SáaHib ad-dukkáan	tamáam, riyaaláin!
Ali	bíshtari. tfáDHDHal. (*gives money*)
SáaHib ad-dukkáan	shúkran. shay tháani?
Ali	laa, laa, laa, shúkran.

 05.06 **Listen again and this time speak Ali's part.**

2 Find the phrases in the conversation which mean:

   a OK, two riyals.   **d** This one costs three riyals.

   b Do you have a cheaper one?   **e** Everything is expensive!

   c (Will you) give me a discount? **f** Anything else?

3 Read the conversation again and answer the questions.

   a What does Ali say about the price of the first item?

   b What does he say about the price of the second item?

   c Why doesn't the shopkeeper want to reduce the price?

   d What is the shopkeeper's last price?

Language discovery

1 Which part of the following phrase means *the-red-one*?

háadha l-míjmar al-áHmar bikám?

2 Which word means *two riyals*?

NOUN/ADJECTIVE PHRASES

There are rules in Arabic about using nouns and adjectives together. First, you will need to distinguish between indefinite and definite words and phrases.

▶ Indefinite words in English are preceded by *a* or *an*, but there is no word for *a* or *an* in Arabic:

| **bait** | *(a) house* | **silsílah** | *(a) necklace* |

▶ Definite words in English are preceded by *the*:

| **al-bait** | *the house* | **as-silsílah** | *the necklace* |

When you use an adjective with a noun to make a phrase:

a the adjective must always follow the noun.

b the adjective must agree in gender (masculine or feminine) and definiteness, *e.g. the-incense-burner, the-red-one.*

Ordinal numbers are the sole exception to this rule.

In Arabic the use or omission of **al-** (*the*) has a powerful effect on the meaning. There are three basic phrase types:

1 no **al-** on either word produces an indefinite phrase:

| **bait jadíid** | *(a) new house* | **silsílah gadíimah** | *(an) old necklace* |

2 **al-** on both words produces a definite phrase:

| **al-bait al-jadíid** | *the new house* |
| **as-silsílah al-gadíimah** | *the old necklace* |

3 **al-** on the noun but not on the adjective produces a sentence that, in English, would contain *is* or *are*, which, as you already know, are not used in Arabic:

| **al-bait jadíid** | *the house (is) new* |
| **as-silsílah gadíimah** | *the necklace (is) old* |

AL-ALWÁAN *THE COLOURS*

 05.07 As you learned in Units 2 and 3, adjectives in Arabic must agree with the gender of the noun they describe. The names of the main colours have slightly different masculine and feminine forms (first form given is masculine, the second feminine).

ázrag/zárga (ázraq/zárqa)	*blue*	**áHmar/Hámra**	*red*
áswad/sóoda	*black*	**ábyaDH/báiDHa**	*white*
áSfar/Sáfra	*yellow*	**ákhDHar/kháDHra**	*green*

Colours ending in **-i** add **-yah** in the feminine form.

burtugáali (burtuqáali)/burtugáaliyah	*orange*
ramáadi/ramáadiyah	*grey*
wárdi/wárdiyah	*pink*
gamíiS ázrag	*a blue shirt* (**gamíiS** is masculine)
zoolíyyah zárga	*a blue carpet* (**zoolíyyah** is feminine)

THE DUAL FORM

When you talk about two of anything in Arabic, you use a special dual form which adds **-áin** to the end of the word (or **-táin** if the word ends in **-ah**). You then don't need to use the word **ithnáin** (m) or **thintáin** (f).

riyáal	*a/one riyal*	**riyaaláin**	*two riyals*
wálad	*a/one boy*	**waladáin**	*two boys*
silsílah	*a/one necklace*	**silsilatáin**	*two necklaces*

> **PRONUNCIATION TIP**
> Note that the stress moves to the end of the word in the dual form.

CURRENCIES OF THE GULF

Bahrain and Kuwait use the **dináar**, which is divided into 1000 **fils**.

The Omani **riyáal** (RO) is divided into 1000 **báiza**.

The Qatari **riyáal** (QR) is divided into 100 **dírham**.

The Saudi **riyáal** (SR) is divided into 100 **hálala**.

The United Arab Emirates use the **dírham** (AED or Dh), which is divided into 100 **fils**.

> **PRONUNCIATION TIP**
> **dináar** and **dirham** are the most common terms for currency types in the Arab world. **dináar** is originally from the Latin *Denarius*, a silver coin used in the Roman Empire from which pre-decimal British money got the symbol D for penny.

NUMBERS 30 TO 1,000,000

05.08 Listen to the numbers and say them out loud.

٣٠	30	thalaathíin
٣٥	35	khámsah wa thalaathíin
٤٠	40	arba:íin
٥٠	50	khamsíin
٦٠	60	sittíin
٧٠	70	sab:íin
٨٠	80	thamaaníin
٩٠	90	tis:íin
٩٩	99	tís:ah wa tis:íin
١٠٠	100	míyyah
١٢٠	120	míyyah w :ashríin
٢٠٠	200	miitáin
٣٠٠	300	thaláath míyyah
٤٠٠	400	árba: míyyah
١٠٠	1000	alf (pl aaláaf)
٢٠٠	2000	alfáin
٣٠٠	3000	thaláthah aaláaf
١٠٠	1,000,000	milyóon (malaayíin)

Remember that Arabic numbers read from left to right, though groups of numbers are still shown right to left, as in these apartment numbers.

Here are two well-known Arabic story titles that include numbers. Can you guess what the stories are from their numbers?

a alf láilah wa láilah
b :áli báaba w al-arba:íin Haráami

PRACTICE 2

1 Are these colours feminine or masculine? Choose the correct form for the items below.

a	zoolíyyah	áHmar/Hámra
b	bánjari	burtugáali/-íyyah
c	gamíiS	ákhDHar/kháDHra
d	bantalóon	áswad/sóoda
e	silsílah	ázrag/zárga

2 You are going on a camping holiday in Fujairah and have seen some camping equipment advertised online. Match the price tags to the prices.

1	Dh89	**5**	Dh97
2	Dh79	**6**	Dh99
3	Dh36	**7**	Dh74
4	Dh25		

a
٩٩ درهم

b ٨٩ درهم

c ٩٧ درهم

d ٣٦ درهم

٧٤ درهم
e

٧٩ درهم
f

٢٥ درهم
g

3 Match the Arabic numbers to their equivalent in English.

a	٩٠	**1**	350
b	٤٥	**2**	725
c	١٠٠	**3**	90
d	٣٥٠	**4**	45
e	٧٢٥	**5**	100

Go further

READING ARABIC

The letters **r** ر and **z** ز (**raa'** and **zaay**) and **s** س and **sh** ش (**siin** and **shiin**) are all Sun letters.

zaay only differs from **raa'** by having one dot above it.

Both these letters are non-joiners, i.e. neither of them joins onto the following letter, and they start on the line and end below it.

siin and **shiin** are identical except that **shiin** has three dots above it. They both join onto a following letter, and are small letters on the line.

end of a word	middle of a word	start of a word	on its own
أخضر **ákhDar** green	بريطانيا **briTáaniya** Britain	رخيص **rakhíiS** cheap	ر **raa'**
موز **móoz** banana	تزلج **tazálluj** skiing	زولية **zoolíyyah** carpet	ز **zaay**
شمس **shams** sun	فستان **fustáan** dress	سبعين **sab:iin** seventy	س **siin**
مشمش **míshmish** apricot	عشرة **:ásharah** ten	شمس **shams** sun	ش **shiin**

Match the transliteration to the Arabic, then find the letters raa' ر and zaay ز, siin س and shin ش in the words below. Do they appear at the beginning (B), middle (M) or end (E) of each word?

	Arabic word		Transliteration
a	درهم	1	ázraq
b	زولية	2	dináar
c	دينار	3	silsílah
d	مجمر	4	:ásharah
e	سلسلة	5	dírham
f	أزرق	6	ramáadi
g	عشرة	7	zoolíiyah
h	رمادي	8	míjimar

Test yourself

05.09 You are on holiday in Dubai and go to the gold **suug** to do some shopping. Play your part in the conversation following the prompts. Remember that *necklace* is a feminine word!

ínta	*Greet the shopkeeper.*
SáaHib ad-dukkáan	w :aláikum as-saláam.
ínta	*Say you want to buy a necklace.*
SáaHib ad-dukkáan	*(he hands you one)* tfáDHDHal.
ínta	*Ask if he has a longer one.*
SáaHib ad-dukkáan	áywa – tfáDHDHal.
ínta	*Say thank you, then ask if it is new.*
SáaHib ad-dukkáan	Táb:an!
ínta	*Ask how much it is.*
SáaHib ad-dukkáan	thaláath míyyah wa khamsíin dírham.
ínta	*Say it's expensive.*
Shopkeeper	kill shay gháali!
ínta	*Say you will buy it.*

SELF CHECK

	I CAN . . .
○	... ask for an item in a shop.
○	... recognize prices online
○	... ask for something different.
○	... say what colour something is.
○	... recognize and use numbers 11 to 1 million.
○	... ask about prices.

In this unit you will learn how to:
» say what you like to eat and drink.
» say what you like and dislike.
» say what you prefer.
» order snacks and drinks.

aish ti-ríid tí-shrab?

My progress tracker

DAY / DATE

Food and drink

You don't have to travel far in the Gulf to find a **dukkáan** (*small shop*) selling **mashruubáat** (*drinks*) and hot or cold **sandwiicháat**, whether in a **mool** (*mall*) in town or at a garage miles from anywhere. In the city, there is almost unlimited choice, and you will find a snack bar or **máT:am** (*restaurant*) on every corner, offering food from all around the world.

Arab hospitality is renowned, and wherever you go you will be offered **gáHwah**, **shaay** or a cold drink, and in a home, maybe some **tamr** (*dates*) or fruit and often **kaik** (*cake*). Arabic coffee is much weaker than Turkish coffee, and is usually flavoured with cardamom. It is served in tiny cups, and your **finjáan** (*coffee cup*) will be refilled until you hand it back, shaking it slightly from side to side. If you are offered fruit or cake, it is considered polite to accept at least one piece, even if you have just had a big meal. When offered dates, take one, three or five, rather than two or four or six – it's just customary to take an odd number!

Find the Arabic word for: **a** drinks   **b** sandwiches

Vocabulary builder

ASKING FOR DRINKS

06.01 Look at these words and phrases and add the missing English words to complete them. Now listen – do they sound like any English words you know?

mashruubáat	*drinks*
gáHwah	*coffee*
shaay	*tea*
... bi-Halíib/bi-l-Halíib	*... with milk*
... bi-dúun Halíib	*... without _____*
súkkar (*or* síkkar)	_____
:aSíir burtugáal	*orange juice*
:aSíir mángu	*mango _____*
:aSíir laimóon	*lemon juice*
... bi-na:náa:	*... _____ mint*
maay	*water*
kóola	_____

NEW EXPRESSIONS

06.02 Look at these expressions, and note their meanings.

aish ti-ríid tí-shrib?	*What do you want to drink?*
ti-Híbb tí-shrib aish?	*What would you like to drink?*
aish :índ-kum min mashruubáat?	*What sorts of drinks do you have?*
	(lit. *what with-you* (pl) *of drinks*)
a-Híbb ...	*I like ...*
maa a-Híbb ...	*I don't like ...*
a-fáDHDHal ...	*I prefer ...*
ána áa-khudh	*I take*
ána báa-khudh	*I'll take*
Táyyib	*OK, fine, good*

Hiwaar 1 *Conversation 1*

06.03 Mohammed is showing Lauren and Anya around Abu Dhabi when they stop at a drinks stall on the Corniche. Listen as you read, then answer the question.

1 What doesn't Anya like?

Most coastal towns and cities in the Gulf have a Corniche – an immaculate seafront promenade lined with palms and flowerbeds, which is perfect for joggers and cyclists during the day and for friends and families to stroll along in the evening.

Mohammed	aish ti-riid-íin ti-shrib-íin ya lóoran?
Lauren	aish :índ-kum min mashruubáat?
SáaHib ad-dukkáan	:índ-na gáhwah, shaay, maay, :aSíir, kóola ... kill shaay!
Lauren	ána báa-khudh shaay bi-l-Halíib min fáDHl-ak.
Mohammed	w ínti ya áanya, aish ti-riid-íin?
Anya	ána maa a-Híbb shaay. aish :índ-kum min :aSíir?
SáaHib ad-dukkáan	:índ-na :aSíir burtugáal wa mángu, wa laimóon.
Anya	ána a-fáDHDHal :aSíir laimóon bi na:náa:.
SáaHib ad-dukkáan	bi-súkkar?
Anya	ná:am, bi-súkkar min fáDHlak.
SáaHib ad-dukkáan	Táyyib. w ínta, aish ti-ríid tí-shrib?
Mohammed	ána a-Híbb :aSíir ... láakin báa-khudh gáhwah.
SáaHib ad-dukkáan	Táyyib.

In some parts of the Gulf, such as Oman, the final **-n** of **ti-riid-íin** is left out, and people say **ti-ríid-i** and **tí-shrib-i** instead.

06.03 **Now listen again and this time speak Anya's part.**

2 Match the questions and answers.

a aish ti-ríid tí-shrib?

b aish :índ-kum min mashruubáat?

c aish :índ-kum min :aSíir?

d ti-ríid laimóon bi-súkkar?

1 :índ-na :aSíir burtugáal wa mángu.

2 ná:am.

3 ána áa-khud gáhwah.

4 :índ-na gáhwah, shaay ...

3 Are the following sentences true (T) or false (F)?

a Lauren has tea with milk.

b Anya likes tea.

c The shopkeeper has three varieties of fruit juice.

d Anya asks for lemon juice with mint.

e Mohammed doesn't like juice.

Language discovery

1 **Which Arabic words mean the same as the following?**
   a What drinks have you got?
   b We have coffee.

2 **Find the expressions that mean:**
   a I like juice   **b** I don't like tea   **c** I prefer coffee

1 HOW TO SAY *I HAVE*

There is no verb *to have* in Arabic. Instead, there is the preposition **:ind**, meaning *with* or *in the possession of*, with the possessive pronoun suffix.

(ána) :ind-i	I have	(níHna) :ind-na	we have
(ínta) :ind-ak	you (m) have	(íntu) :índ-kum	you (pl) have
(ínti) :índ-ich	you (f) have		
(húwwa) :ind-uh	he (it) has	(húmma) :ind -hum	they have
(híyya) :ind-ha	she (it) has		

> **PRONUNCIATION TIP**
> In spoken Arabic, there's no difference between masculine and feminine in the plural.

It is common, but not essential, to say the subject or person before **:ind**.

(ána) :índ-i sayyáarah.   *I have a car.* (lit. *(I) with-me (is) (a) car.*)

áHmad :índ-uh marsáidis?   *Does Ahmed have a Mercedes?*
(lit. *Ahmed with-him (is) (a) Mercedes?*)

laa, :índ-uh toyóota.   *No, he has a Toyota.* (lit. *no, with-him (is) (a) Toyota.*)

To say that you don't have an item, use **maa** (*not*) before the preposition.

áHmad maa :índ-uh marsáidis.   *Ahmed doesn't have a Mercedes.*

2 LIKES, DISLIKES AND PREFERENCES

To say what you like, use the stem of the verb *to like*, **-Hibb**, with the present tense prefixes and/or endings.

ána a-Híbb ash-shaay.   *I like (the) tea.*

If you don't like something, again you use **maa** (*not*) before the verb:

(ána) maa a-Híbb al-Halíib.   *(I) don't like (the) milk.*

To say you prefer something, use the verb stem **-fáDHDHal**:

ti-fáDHDHal gáhwah?   *Do you prefer coffee?*

áywa, a-fáDHDHal gáHwah.   *Yes, I prefer coffee.*

> **PRONUNCIATION TIP**
>
> With **a-fáDHDHal**, take care to pronounce both **DH**s – just leave a slight hesitation between each **DH** to be sure, as you would in *with this*.

PRACTICE 1

1 Match the Arabic to the English for each drink.

a	shaay	**1**	mango juice
b	gáHwah	**2**	water
c	:aSíir burtugáal	**3**	coffee
d	maay	**4**	tea without sugar
e	:aSíir mángu	**5**	cola
f	:aSíir laimóon	**6**	tea
g	shaay bi-Halíib	**7**	tea with sugar
h	shaay bidúun súkkar	**8**	lemon juice
i	shaay bi-súkkar	**9**	tea with milk
j	kóola	**10**	orange juice

2 Match the Arabic to its English meaning.

a	aish :ind-ak fi sh-shánTah?	**1**	They have a boy and a girl.
b	:índ-na waladáin	**2**	Has she got a new bag?
c	:índ-ha shánTah jadíidah?	**3**	I have a big car.
d	ána :índ-i sayyáarah kabíirah	**4**	What sort of food have you got?
e	húmma :índ-hum wálad wa bint	**5**	We have two boys/sons.
f	aish :índ-kum min ákil?	**6**	What have you got in the bag?

3 Complete each sentence by adding the correct Arabic word.

a	muHámmad wa faríida _____ wálad wa bint.	**1**	:índ-na
b	náasir _____ sayyáarah saríi:ah.	**2**	:índ-hum
c	níHna maa _____ mashruubáat.	**3**	:índ-kum;
d	íntu _____ gáhwah aw shaay?	**4**	:índ-uh

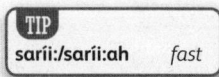

> **TIP**
> **saríi:/saríi:ah**   *fast*

Listen and understand

 1 06.04 **Listen to these people ask for drinks. Which drink does each speaker want to order?**

a orange juice   **c** coffee   **e** water

b tea with sugar   **d** milk   **f** cola light

1 ___ 2 ___ 3 ___ 4 ___ 5 ___ 6 ___

> **TIP**
> **báarid**   *cold (things)*   **láait**   *light, diet*

 2 06.05 **Listen to find out what the speakers prefer. Choose i or ii.**

a i shaay	**ii** gáHwah
b i :aSíir burtugáal	**ii** :aSíir laimóon
c i shaay bi-súkkar	**ii** shaay bidúun súkkar
d i Halíib	**ii** maay

 3 Now say whether or not you like each item in exercise 1.

FOOD

 06.06 **Listen and repeat. Then add the missing English words.**

wajbaat khafíifah	*snacks*
sandwíich (-áat)	*sandwich*
báiDHah (baiDH)	*egg (eggs)*
dajáaj	*chicken*
jíb(i)n	*cheese*
bárgar/bárghar	*burger*
má:a	*with*
baTáaTa/chibs	*chips/fries*
SálaTah	*salad*
khubz	*bread*
faláafil	_____ *(fried bean snack)*
bi-TaHíinah	*with tahini (sesame paste) dip*
bi-HúmmuS	*with* _____ *dip*
kaik	_____

> **TIP**
> Say **ya jamáa:ah!** as a friendly way to address a group of friends or people you know well. It means *Hey, everyone!*

NEW EXPRESSIONS

ána jaw:áan/jaw:áanah.	*I am hungry.*
ínta jaw:áan?	*Are you hungry?* (to a man)
ínti jaw:áanah?	*Are you hungry?* (to a woman)
íntu jaw:aaníin?	*Are you hungry?* (pl)
aish :índ-hum min ákil?	*What have they got to eat?*
a:Tíini ...	*Give (to) me ...*
ána nabáti/nabatiah.	*I am vegetarian/vegan.*
:indi Hasasiyya min (al-qamh / al-láaktuz / al-mukasarat).	*I am allergic to (wheat/lactose/nuts).*
:indi maráad as-sukkari.	*I am diabetic.*
ána la akal al-luhum / muntajat al-álban.	*I don't eat meat/dairy products.*

> **TIP**
> During the Islamic month of Ramadan, most Muslims do not eat or drink anything between the hours of sunrise and sunset. It is considerate not to consume food or drink conspicuously in front of them during the day.

al-Hiin door-ak! *Now your turn!*

How would a man say the following? *I'm hungry! I'll take a burger with fries, please.*

Hiwáar 2 *Conversation 2*

06.07 *Mohammed and some friends are going to order a takeaway delivery online so they look at a menu. First listen, then answer the question.*

1   What food do they decide to order?

Mohammed	íntu jaw:aaníin?
Fatima wa Nasser	háiwa, shwáyya.
Mohammed	aish ti-riid-úun? aish :índ-hum min ákil, yaa náasir?
Nasser	fiih sandwiicháat, SalaTáat, bárgar ... :índ-hum kill shay!
Mohammed	aish ti-Hibb-íin, yaa fáaTimah?
Fatima	ána a-Híbb SálaTah bi-d-dajáaj máːa chibs.
Mohammed	zain. ti-ríid táa-kul aish ya náasir?
Nasser	maa a-ríid SálaTah. a:Tíini sandwíich bi-l-jíbin. wa muHámmad, aish ti-ríid táa-kul?
Mohammed	ána báakhudh bárgar. ya jamáaːah! ti-riid-úun khubz wa Húmmus?
All	Táb:an!

78

TIP

háiwa (or **hái**) is a variant of **aywa**.

 06.07 **Listen again, this time speaking the part of Mohammed.**

2 Match each expression in Arabic to its English meaning.

a	aish :índ-hum min ákil?	**1**	Of course.
b	ti-ríid táa-kul aish?	**2**	Give me a sandwich.
c	a:Tíini sandwíich.	**3**	What food have they got?
d	Táb:an.	**4**	I don't want salad.
e	maa a-ríid SálaTah.	**5**	What do you want to eat? (to a man)

Language discovery

Find the following in the conversation.

1 Are you (pl) hungry?
2 What do you (pl) want?
3 What do you want? (to a man)
4 Do you (pl) want bread?

Now cover up your answers, and see if you can say them again without looking at the conversation.

1 PLURALS OF ADJECTIVES

To describe more than one person in Arabic, add the ending **-íin** to the adjective. There is no distinction for masculine or feminine.

:íntu jaw:aaníin?	*Are you (pl) hungry?*
áywa, níHna wáajid jaw:aaníin	*Yes, we are very hungry*
w :aTshaaníin!	*and thirsty!*

TIP

:aTsháan/:aTsháanah	*thirsty (m/f)*

2 SAYING WHAT YOU WANT

a-ríid	*I want*	**na-ríid**	*we want*
ti-ríid	*you* (m) *want*	**ti-riid-úun**	*you* (pl) *want*
ti-riid-íin	*you* (f) *want*		
yi-ríid	*he wants*	**yi-riid-úun**	*they want*
ti-ríid	*she wants*		

PRACTICE 2

1 Match the Arabic to the English.

a	sandwíich bi-d-dajáaj	**1**	burger
b	sandwíich bi-l-jíbin	**2**	fries
c	sandwíich bi-l-baiDH	**3**	cheese sandwich
d	bárgar	**4**	salad
e	baTáaTa	**5**	chicken sandwich
f	SálaTah	**6**	egg sandwich

2 What does each person prefer to eat?
   a ána afáDHDHal sandwíich bi-l-jibn
   b ána afáDHDHal bárgar má:a baTáaTa
   c ána a-fáDHDHal faláafil wa Hummus

3 Match each question to its correct answer.

a	aish ti-ríid tí-shrab?	**1**	a-ríid sandwíich bi-l-jíbin.
b	ti-riid-úun gáHwah aw shaay?	**2**	a-ríid áshrib kóola.
c	aish ti-riid-íin min sandwiicháat?	**3**	na-ríid gáHwah min fáDHlich.

4 Your friend Ali has dropped by. How would you ask him these questions? Match the Arabic to its English meaning.

a	Are you thirsty?	**1**	ti-ríid sandwíich?
b	What would you like to drink?	**2**	ti-fáDHDHal shaay aw gáhwah?
c	Do you prefer tea or coffee?	**3**	bi-l-jibin aw bi-d-dajáaj?
d	With milk or sugar?	**4**	ínta :aTsháan?
e	Would you like a sandwich?	**5**	ti-ríid tí-shrib aish?
f	Cheese or chicken?	**6**	bi-Halíib aw bi-súkkar?
g	Are you vegetarian?	**7**	:indak maráad as-sukkari?
h	Are you diabetic?	**8**	Hal intá nabáti?

5 Ali has brought some friends with him. How would you ask them all the same questions? Remember to use the plural form throughout.

Go further

READING ARABIC

Two pairs of letters – **S** ص and **D** ض (**Saad** and **Daad**), and **T** ط and **DH** ظ (**Taa'** and **DHaa'**) – are all Sun letters. They are all joiners, and all begin looking like an egg on its side.

The second letter of each pair has one dot above it.

▶ **Saad** and **Daad** have a flourish in the separate and final forms.
▶ **Taa'** and **DHaa'** have no flourish – instead, they have an upright stick added to the left side of the egg.

end of a word	middle of a word	start of a word	on its own
رخيص **rakhíiS** *cheap*	عصير **:aSíir** *juice*	صغير **Saghíir** *small*	ص **Saad**
بيض **baiD** *eggs*	أخضر **ákhDar** *green*	ضيف **Daif** *guest*	ض **Daad**
وسط **wásaT** *middle*	مطعم **máT:am** *restaurant*	طعام **Ta:áam** *food*	ط **Taa'**
حظ **HaDHDH** *luck*	نظيف **naDHíif** *clean*	أبو ظبي **ábu DHábi** *Abu Dhabi*	ظ **DHaa'**

> **TIP**
>
> Remember, the letter **Daad** is usually pronounced like the letter **DHaa'** in the Gulf, so **baiDH** (*eggs*) is actually spelled **baiD** in written form.

1 Look at the Arabic words and find the letters **Saad** and **Daad**, **Taa'** and **DHaa'**. Do they appear at the beginning (B), middle (M) or end (E) of these words?

	Arabic		Transliteration and meaning
a	قطر	1	ábu **DH**ábi (*Abu Dhabi*)
b	طيب	2	á**S**far (*yellow*)
c	قميص	3	bái**D**ah (*an egg*)
d	الظهران	4	qamíi**S** (*a shirt*)
e	أبو ظبي	5	ar**D** (*land*)
f	بيضة	6	a**DH-DH**ahrán (*Dhahran*)
g	أصفر	7	qá**T**ar (*Qatar*)
h	أرض	8	**T**áyyib (*fine, ok*)

2 Now match the Arabic words to their transliteration.

3 Read each sign and match it to its meaning. Remember to look for letters you have learned in this unit.

a مطعم

b خروج فقط

c ممنوع التصوير

1 *exit only* (**kharúuj fáqaT**)
2 *no photography* (**mamnúu: at-taSwíir**)
3 *restaurant* (**máT:am**)

Test yourself

You go into a café for a snack and a drink. Following the prompts, give the most appropriate reply.

SáaHib ad-dukkáan	masáa' al-khair.
ínta	*Reply appropriately and ask what they've got to drink.*
SáaHib ad-dukkáan	:índ-na shaay, gáhwah, :aSíir, kóola ...
ínta	*Ask what kinds of juice they have.*
SáaHib ad-dukkáan	:índ-na :aSíir burtugáal wa tufráH, wa laimóon.
ínta	*Say you'll take an apple juice. Ask what kinds of sandwiches they have.*
SáaHib ad-dukkáan	fiih sandwiicháat bi-l-jíbin, bi-d-dajáaj, bi-l-báiDH, wa fiih bárgar.
ínta	*Ask him to give you a burger and fries.*
SáaHib ad-dukkáan	má:a SálaTah?
ínta	*Tell him no, without salad.*
SáaHib ad-dukkáan	*(a few minutes later)* tfáDHDHal.
ínta	*Make an appropriate reply.*

R2

Review: Units 4–6

1 Complete each Arabic sentence, saying out loud the time shown.

  a 3:00 = as-sáa:ah _____.

  b 5:10 = as-sáa:ah khámsah _____ :áshar.

  c 7:30 = as-sáa:ah _____ wa _____.

  d 9:45 = as-sáa:ah :ásharah _____ rúba:.

2 Do these times occur in the morning (a.m.) or evening (p.m.)?

  a as-sáa:ah khámsah aS-SúbaH.

  b as-sáa:ah thaláathah fi l-lail.

  c as-sáa:ah thintáin ba:d aDH-DHuhr.

  d as-sáa:ah sáb:ah aS-SúbaH.

3 You have just arrived at your hotel in Doha. It's hot and you fancy a swim. Ask the receptionist if there is a pool in the hotel.

4 Rank the days of the week in order from Sunday (1) to Saturday (7).

  a yoom al-júma:ah

  b yoom ath-thaláathah

  c yoom al-árba:ah

  d yoom as-sabt

  e yoom al-áHad

  f yoom al-khamíis

  g yoom al-ithnáin

5 Unjumble each sentence so it makes sense in Arabic. Then say each sentence out loud.

  a kam as-síinima as-sáa:ah tíftaH?

  b as-sáa:ah yibánnid al-máT:am kam?

  c wa al-mool as-sáa:ah nuss yíftaH tís:ah.

  d fi l-lail al-másbaH as-sáa:ah sáb:ah yibánnid.

6 Match each number in Arabic to its correct numeral in the box. Careful! Two more numerals than necessary have been provided.

٨٧	٥٣	٢٣٠	٢٠٠٠
٢٩	٤٥	٣٥	٩٢

a thaláathah wa khamsíin _____
b khámsah wa arba:íin _____
c miitáin wa thalathíin _____
d tís:ah wa :ashríin _____
e sáb:ah wa thamaníin _____
f alfáin _____

Now say these numbers out loud in Arabic and English.

7 All Arabic nouns are either masculine or feminine. Complete these statements on grammar by selecting the correct Arabic word.
   a For masculine nouns you use **húwwa/híyya** to say *it (is)*, and **háadha/háadhi** to say *this (is)*.
   b For feminine nouns you use **húwwa/híyya** to say *it (is)*, and **háadha/háadhi** to say *this (is)*.

8 Decide whether each of these nouns is masculine (M) or feminine (F), then give the correct English meaning of each.
   a khaatim   **c** míjmar   **e** fustáan
   b silsílah   **d** biTaagah (SIM)   **f** gamíiS

9 Lara did the homework for her Arabic course in a rush and forgot to change **háadha** to **háadhi** for the feminine words. She also got some of her adjective endings muddled up. Help Lara by suggesting corrections, where appropriate. Did she get any right?
   a *háadha zooliyyah jamíil.*   ❑ _____
   b *háadha míjmar kabíir.*   ❑ _____
   c *háadha finjáan rakhíiSah.*   ❑ _____
   d *haadha silsílah Tawíil.*   ❑ _____

Now translate each sentence into English.

10 Write the meaning of these adjectives in English. Then match each adjective to its comparative form in Arabic.

a	kabíir	_____	**1**	ágSar
b	Saghíir	_____	**2**	áTwal
c	rakhíiS	_____	**3**	áSghar
d	gháali	_____	**4**	ákbar
e	gaSíir	_____	**5**	árkhaS
f	Tawíil	_____	**6**	ághla
g	jamíil	_____	**7**	ájmal

11 Ask out loud in Arabic for a different item using the comparative adjectives in the previous exercise. Use the masculine form for each.

Example: :índ-ak tháani árkhaS? (*Do you have a cheaper one?*)

12 Add the correct ending for the preposition :**índ** (*with*), following the prompts in English.

a	:índ _____	I have (lit. with-me, etc.)
b	:índ _____	he has
c	:índ _____	we have
d	:índ _____	they have
e	:índ _____	you (f) have

13 Match the English to the Arabic.

a	:índ-ak gamíiS ábyaDH?	**1**	This is a blue car.
b	:háadhi sayyáarah zárgah.	**2**	Where is the green apple?
c	wain at-tufáaHah al-kháDHra?	**3**	I want to buy the black car.
d	a-ríid a-shtári as-sayyáarah as-sóoda.	**4**	Do you have a white shirt?

14 You are in a café. Ask the server in Arabic for these items.

a I'd like _____ please.

b I'll take _____ please.

c Give me _____ please.

15 Which is the odd one out and why?
 a al-ithnáin   as-sabt   al-áHad   al-fúndug
 b khamsíin   saba:íin   thaláathah   :ashríin
 c áHmar   zoolíyyah   burtugáali   áswad
 d :aSíir laimóon   kaik   faláafil   khubz

16 Mustafa got a speeding ticket while driving along this road.
 How fast was he going?
 a 40 km/h   **b** 50km/h   **c** 60km/h

17 You see these signs while shopping. Match them to their transliteration and English meaning.

a المخرج   _____

b نعناع   _____

c مفتوح   _____

d تنزيلات   _____

e شاي   _____

f تفاح   _____

g طماطم   _____

h برتقال   _____

A	tanziiláat	1	apple
B	TamáaTim	2	tea
C	burtuqáal	3	exit
D	al-makhraj	4	mint
E	tufáaH	5	orange
F	shaay	6	tomato
G	na:náa:	7	open
H	maftúuH	8	reductions/discounts

7

In this unit you will learn how to:
» ask for places in a town.
» ask where places are.
» ask for and give directions.
» direct a taxi driver to your destination.

fi l-madíinah

My progress tracker

DAY / DATE

Getting around the city

Most Gulf cities were laid out during the 1970s and 1980s, mainly as a result of the rocketing price of oil. Development is ongoing throughout the region and many cities are ultra-contemporary, with clusters of **abráaj** (*towers*) of dizzying heights and futuristic designs crowding the skyline. In contrast, others are more traditional, their history and heritage evident at every turn. Each district has its own **másjid** (*mosque*), often more than one, and it won't be long before you become accustomed to the sound of the **adháan** (*Islamic call to prayer*) five times a day. Cities such as Dubai and Sharjah grew up around creeks, and these and other coastal cities have a **míina** (*port* or *harbour*) and a **suug as-sámak**. And, wherever you are, you are sure to stumble across a **mool** or two!

Getting around is fun once you have mastered a few simple phrases such as **wain as-suug?** (*Where is the market?*) and **fiih dukkáan garíib min hína?** (*Is there a shop near here?*) If you know your **yisáar** (*left*) from your **yamíin** (*right*), you will soon find your way around **wásaT al-madíinah** (*the centre of town*) without getting lost.

If **sámak** means *fish*, what is a **suug as-sámak**?

Vocabulary builder

07.01 Listen, then complete the English translations by adding the missing words.

fi l-madíinah	*in the city*
al-báHar	*the sea/beach*
al-khoor	*the creek*
al-jísir	*the bridge*
al-másjid	*the _____*
al-mátHaf	*the museum*
al-maTáar	*the airport*
*ash-sháari:	*the street*
*aS-Saydalíiyah	*the pharmacy*
*as-súubermarkit	*the _____*
suug *as-sámak	*the fish _____*

> **PRONUNCIATION TIP**
> *Remember that all these words begin with a Sun letter, so the **laam** in **al-** (*the*) is silent, and the first letter is clearly doubled.

al-ittijaháat	*directions*
ruuH	*go!* (to a man)
rúuHi	*go!* (to a woman)
liff	*turn!* (to a man)
líffi	*turn!* (to a woman)
khudh	*take!* (to a man)
khúdhi	*take!* (to a woman)
síidah	*straight on*
yamíin	*right*
yisaar (*also* shimáal)	*left*
:ála l-yisáar	*on the _____*
:ála l-yamíin	*on the _____*

NEW EXPRESSIONS

07.02 Listen and repeat, trying to match the speakers' pronunciation.

law samáHt	*please, excuse me* (to a man)
law samáHti	*please, excuse me* (to a woman)
garíib/garíibah (qaríib/qaríibah)	*near* (m/f)
fiih bank garíib min hína?	*Is there a bank near here?*

al-bank ba:íid :an hína?	*(Is) the bank far from here?*
tá:raf sháari: ...?	*Do you know ... street?*
maa á:raf.	*I don't know.*
ba:dáin	*then, after that*
muu ákthar	*not more*
maa fiih	*there isn't*

Hiwaar 1 *Conversation 1*

07.03 *Suresh is spending the afternoon in Muscat and needs to find a bank. He asks a passer-by for help. First listen, then answer the question.*

1 What is the first direction the man gives to Suresh?

Suresh	law samáHt, fiih bank garíib min hína?
rajjáal	áywa fiih. tá:raf sháari: al-bustáan?
Suresh	laa, maa á:raf.
rajjáal	zain. ruuH síidah wa ba:dáin liff yamíin. al-bank :ála l-yisáar.
Suresh	al-bank ba:íid :an hína?
rajjáal	laa laa, húwwa garíib. khams dagáayig bass, muu ákthar.
Suresh	shúkran. wa fiih baríid garíib min hína?
rajjáal	laa, maa fiih.
Suresh	shúkran.
rajjáal	:áfwan

> **TIP**
>
> You already know how to say *please* (**min fáDHl-ak/-ich**). The phrase **law samáHt** (to a man) and **law samáHti** (to a woman) is a more polite or formal way of saying *please*, and is often used to mean *excuse me* when you want to attract someone's attention, such as in a restaurant.

---

2 Match the Arabic to the English.

a	left	**1**	yamíin
b	near	**2**	síidah
c	right	**3**	garíib
d	straight on	**4**	yisáar

3 Find the Arabic phrases that mean:

a No, I don't know.
b Go straight.
c Then turn right.
d Is the bank far from here?

4 Are these statements true (T) or false (F)?

a Suresh knows where al-Bustaan street is.
b First he must go straight.
c The bank is on the left.
d The bank is ten minutes away.

Language discovery

1 Find the Arabic phrases that mean:

a Is there a post office near here?
b No, there isn't.

2 Find the Arabic phrase that means *Go straight.*

1 *THERE IS* AND *THERE ARE*

It is very easy to say *there is* and *there are* in Arabic – just use the word **fiih**. The **h** is silent, but is written this way to distinguish it from the word **fii** meaning *in*. Remember, there is no word for *a* or *an*.

fiih fúndug.	*There is a hotel.*
fiih fúndug fii dubáy.	*There is a hotel in Dubai.*

To express *there is not* or *there are not*, you say **maa fiih**.

maa fiih fúndug garíib min hína.	*There isn't a hotel near here.*

> **REGIONAL VARIATIONS OF FIIH**
> Mainly in Bahrain you will hear the use of **hast** instead of **fiih**, and in Kuwait and Iraq people say **áku**.

2 TELLING PEOPLE TO DO SOMETHING

These forms of the verb (known as imperatives) are frequently used in giving directions. Those you have met in this unit are:

ruuH!	*go!*
liff!	*turn!*
khudh!	*take!*

Imperative verb forms have to be altered according to the person spoken to, so you add **-i** if you are talking to a woman and **-u** if you are talking to more than one person of either gender.

	masculine	feminine	plural
go	**ruuH**	**rúuHi**	**rúuHu**
turn	**liff**	**líffi**	**líffu**
take	**khudh**	**khúdhi**	**khúdhu**

PRACTICE 1

1 **There are five places about town mentioned in this word-snake. Can you find them? Then mark the stress on each word where appropriate.**

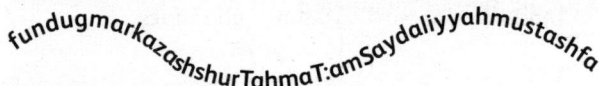

fundugmarkazashshurTahmaT:amSaydaliyyahmustashfa

2 **Match each direction to its correct symbol.**

   a síidah   **1** ←

   b yisáar   **2** →

   c yamíin   **3** ↑

3 **Match the Arabic to the English.**

   a laa, maa fiih.   **1** Where is the airport?

   b al-maTáar min wain?   **2** Is there a restaurant near here?

   c fiih máT:am garíib min hína?   **3** Go straight then turn left.

   d ruuH síidah wa ba:dáin liff yisáar. **4** No, there isn't.

4 **Which imperative verb would you use to complete each sentence?**

   a ruuH/liff yisáar.

   b ruuH/liff síidah.

   c ruuH/liff yamíin.

 5 **You are out and about in town. Ask a passer-by if each of these places is nearby. Remember to use garíibah for feminine words.**

> **PRONUNCIATION TIP**
> You don't need to use **al-** as you are asking for *a* restaurant rather than *the* restaurant.
> Example: **fiih maTáar garíib min hína?**   *Is there a restaurant near here?*

a	post office (m)	**e**	hotel (m)
b	hospital (f)	**f**	pharmacy (f)
c	police station (m)	**g**	school (f)
d	museum (m)	**h**	fish market (m)

6 **Now repeat exercise 5, this time asking if each place is far from here. Remember to use ba:íidah for feminine nouns.**

Example: al-maTáar ba:íid :an hína?   *Is the airport far from here?*

Listen and understand

1 07.04 **Listen to these people talk about places in town. Where does each person want to go? Choose from the following list, then say if there is (fiih) or isn't (maa fiih) such a place in town.**

> market   cinema   museum   pharmacy
> shop   hospital   hotel

a	_____	e	_____
b	_____	f	_____
c	_____	g	_____
d	_____		

2 07.05 **Where are the speakers going and how do they get there? For example, to get to A the speaker must use Directions 3.**

A

B

C

D

1 ↑←   **2** ↑   **3** → ←   **4** → ↑

a	_____	c	_____
b	_____	d	_____

NEW EXPRESSIONS

07.06 **First listen, then add the missing words.**

al-fúndug min wain?	*Where is the _____?*
kaif a-rúuH al-fúndug?	*How do I get to _____?*
áwwal yamíin	*(the) first _____*
tháani yiSáar	*(the) second _____*
:ind ad-duwwáar	*at the roundabout*
laa tísra:!	*Don't speed up!*
muu mushkílah!	*No problem!*

Hiwáar 2 *Conversation 2*

07.07 *Anya is lost in Ruwi because the taxi driver can't find her hotel. She opens the window to ask a passer-by. First listen, then answer the question.*

1 What is the name of Anya's hotel?

Anya	law samáHt, fúndug ash-shams min wain?
rajjáal	*(scratching his chin)* khallíini afákkir ... rúuHi síida, wa :ind ad-duwwáar líffi yamíin wa ba:dáin khúdhi tháani sháari: :ála l-yamíin.
Anya	zain, wa ba:dáin?
rajjáal	fúndug ash-shams bá:d khamsíin mítir, jamb máT:am aS-SaHaráa'.
Anya	shúkran. wa kaif arúuH al-báHar min al-fúndug?
rajjáal	al-báHar wáajid garíib – min al-fúndug khúdhi áakhir sháari: :ála l-yisáar. yá:ani ... thaláath dagáayig bass.
Anya	Hayyáa-k Alláah.
rajjáal	fii amáan Alláah.
(The taxi driver speeds up.)	
Anya	*(shouting)* shwáyya shwáyya, laa tísra:!
sawwáag	muu mushkílah!

> **TIP**
>
> | | |
> |---|---|
> | **sawwáag (at-táaksi)** | *(taxi) driver* |
> | **rajjáal** | *man* |
> | **khallíini afákkir** | *let me think* |

2 What does Anya say to the passer-by at the end?

> **TIP**
>
> **Hayyáa-k Alláah** is a well-wishing phrase, literally meaning *God give you life*. It can mean *goodbye* or *thank you*, depending on the context. The response **fii amáan Alláah** means *May God keep you safe*.

07.07 **Listen again and speak Anya's part.**

3 Complete the notes for Anya's directions in English.

Go _____, then at the _____, turn _____, then take the _____ street on the _____. The Sun Hotel is after _____ meters, next to the Desert _____.

Language discovery

Find the phrases in the conversation which mean:
   a take the second street on the right
   b next to the Desert Restaurant

1 ORDINAL NUMBERS

Ordinal numbers tell us what order things are in, i.e. *first, second, third* and so on. They are commonly used when giving directions.

áwwal	*first*	**sáadis**	*sixth*
tháani	*second*	**sáabi:**	*seventh*
tháalith	*third*	**tháamin**	*eighth*
ráabi:	*fourth*	**táasi:**	*ninth*
kháamis	*fifth*	**:áashir**	*tenth*

You might also need the word **áakhir**, meaning *last*, as in **áakhir sháari: :ála l-yamíin** (*last street on the right*).

Unlike normal adjectives, which come after the noun, ordinal numbers can sometimes appear before the noun, especially when giving directions.

2 PREPOSITIONS

Prepositions are words that tell us the position of something.

Arabic	English	Example
fii	*in*	**fi l-madíinah*** *in the city*
:ála	*on*	**:ála l-yisáar*** *on the left*
:ind	*at, by*	**:ind ad-duwwáar** *at the roundabout*
jamb	*next to*	**jamb al-máT:am** *next to the restaurant*
gábil (qábil)	*before*	**gábil al-jísir** *before the bridge*
bá:d	*after*	**bá:d al-jísir** *after the bridge*
amáam	*in front of*	**amáam al-bait** *in front of the house*
wára	*behind*	**wára s-sayyáarah*** *behind the car*
foog	*up, above*	**íTla: foog** *go up*; **foog ad-dukkáan** *above the shop*
táH(i)t	*down, under*	**ínzil taH(i)t** *go down*; **táH(i)t al-jísir** *under the bridge*

TIP
*If a word beginning with **al-** (*the*) follows **fii**, **:ála** or **wára**, the two words slide into each other and the **a** in **al-** (*the*) is not pronounced.

PRACTICE 2

1 Match the Arabic to the English.

a	fii	**1**	on
b	gábil	**2**	behind
c	:ála	**3**	in
d	foog	**4**	under
e	jamb	**5**	above
f	taHt	**6**	at
g	wára	**7**	before
h	:ind	**8**	next to

2 How would you say the following to a man?
   a Take the first street on the right.
   b Take the third street on the left.
   c Take the fourth street on the right then turn left.
   d Take the second street on the right then go straight.
   e At the roundabout turn left.

3 Repeat exercise 2, but respond as if you were talking to a woman.

 4 07.08 Listen to these speakers, then answer the questions.
  a Where does he want to go?
  b What directions is he given?
  c How far is it?
  d Where is it exactly?

> **TIP**
> **bitshúufi** *you (f) will see*

 5 How would you say the following in Arabic? Some of the words you will need are given in the box. Remember there is no word for *is*.

Example: a al-wálad fi l-máT:am.

al-wálad	al-baríid	aS-Saydalíyyah	al-másjid
as-sayyáarah	al-fúndug	as-síinima	al-mátHaf	al-jísir

  a The boy is in the restaurant.
  b The cinema is after the police station.
  c The post office is before the supermarket.
  d The pharmacy is next to the museum.
  e The car is under the bridge.
  f The hotel is after the mosque.

Go further

📖 **READING ARABIC**

The letters ع (**:ain**) and **gh** غ (**ghain**) are identical in shape, a big bulge below a smaller bulge, except that **ghain** has a dot above it. Learn them as a pair and, as with all the other letters you have learned, practice spotting and distinguishing between them whenever you see written Arabic. This is what they look like on their own, at the start, in the middle and at the end of a word.

end of a word	middle of a word	start of a word	on its own
سريع **saríi:** *fast*	بعد **ba:d** *after*	عنب **:ínab** *grapes*	ع **:ain**
مبلغ **máblagh** *amount*	صغير **Saghíir** *small*	غالي **gháali** *expensive*	غ **ghain**

1 Complete the English meaning or transliteration for the Arabic words in the table.

	English meaning	Transliteration	Arabic
a		sháari:	شارع
b	language		لغة
c		:ála	على
d		ba:dáin	بعدين
e	juice		عصير
f		gháali	غالي
g	Oman		عمان
h		baghdáad	بغداد

2 How would you write the title at the top of the Arabic script column in Arabic script?

3 Now highlight the letters :ain and ghain in each Arabic word in the table.

4 You see these signs at a petrol station. Which sign says:

   a :áadi   *regular (petrol)*

   b mamnúu: at-tadkhíin   *no smoking*

1

2

Test yourself

1 **Complete this conversation by adding the correct words from the box.**

fiih	rúuH	samáHt	tháani	ba:d
yamíin	:ála	as-suug	wain	maa

ínta	law _____, al-mátHaf al-isláami min _____?
rajjáal	_____ síida, wa :ind ad-duwwáar liff _____ wa
	ba:dáin khudh _____ sháari: _____ l-yamíin.
ínta	zain, wa ba:dáin?
rajjáal	al-mátHaf _____ khamsíin mítir, jamb _____.
ínta	wa _____ bank garíib min hína?
rajjáal	laa, _____ fiih.

2 **How would you ask the following in Arabic?**
  a Is there is a restaurant near here?
  b Where is the sea?
  c How do I get to the cinema from here?

3 **How would you say the following in Arabic?**
  a Go straight on. (to a man)
  b Turn left then go straight. (to a woman)
  c Go straight then take the second right. (to a man)
  d No, there isn't a bank near here.
  e The fish market is next to the harbour.

SELF CHECK

	I CAN . . .
○	... ask for places in a town.
○	... ask where places are.
○	... ask for and give directions.
○	... direct a taxi driver to my destination.

8

In this unit you will learn how to:
» book and buy travel tickets.
» hire a car.
» buy petrol and deal with simple car problems.

li-wain?

My progress tracker →

DAY / DATE

Getting out and about

Thanks to heavily subsidized **banzíin** (*petrol*) prices in the Gulf states, travel by **at-táaksi** is cheap and easy and you won't have to wait long for one in most major cities. Many taxis have meters these days, but if not, before getting inside, you should ask the price – **tirúuH as-suug bikám?** (*How much to the market?*) Dubai has a clean and modern **mítru** system, and like the city's buses, fully air-conditioned. In some Gulf countries, **baaS** (*bus*) services are very sporadic, but in others there is a well-established bus network. Waiting at the **máwgif al-baaS** can get a little hot during summer months, but some are enclosed and air-conditioned. Long-distance buses are a cheap and convenient way to travel across the region or of course you can go by **Tayyáarah** (*plane*). Metro and bus stations are generally accessible for **al-karasi al-mutaHarikah** (*wheelchairs*) and people with mobility issues, with **al-miS:ad** (*elevators*) and **masarat írshádiah** (*guide tracks*) for the visually impaired. All metro carriages have **amakan khasah limustakhdimi al-karasi al-mutaHrikah** (designated spaces for wheelchair users).

Find the Arabic for: **a** metro   **b** bus stop

Vocabulary builder

08.01 First read, then add the missing English words. Then listen and repeat.

as-sáfar	*travel*
baaS (-áat)	*bus*
sayyáarah (-áat)	*car*
táaksi (-yáat)	_____
giTáar (qiTáar) (-áat)	*train*
mítru	_____
Tayyáarah (-áat)	*plane*
tádhkarah (tadháakir)	*ticket (tickets)*
dhiháab	*one way* (lit. *going*)
dhiháab w iyáab	*return* (lit. *going and coming back*)
mubáasharatan	*direct*
al-karáasi al-mutHárikah	*wheelchairs*
al-míS:ad	*elevators*
masaráat irsháadiyah	*guide tracks (for the visually impaired)*
khasah li-mustákhdimi al-karáasi al-mutaHárikah	*designated spaces for wheelchair users*

NEW EXPRESSIONS

08.02 First read, then add the missing English words. Then listen and repeat these expressions.

fiih baaS yirúuH ad-dóoHah?	*Is there a _____ that goes to Doha?*
fiih baaS yirúuH ...	*There is (a) bus (which) goes ...*
mubáasharatan	*direct* (lit. *there (is) bus it-goes directly*)
al-baaS yíTla: as-sáa:ah thintáin	*the bus leaves at _____ o'clock*
máta?	*When?*
yóoSal (m) al-baaS	*the bus arrives*
tóoSal (f) aT-Tayyáarah	*the _____ arrives*
Hagg báakir (báachir)	*for tomorrow*
múmkin ádfa: bi l-kart?	*Can I pay by card?*
múmkin ádfa: bi l-háatif al-maHmúul?	*Can I pay by phone?*
múmkin	*it's possible*

> **TIP**
> Now that you have got used to the verb prefixes and suffixes, these and the stress in each word will only be shown in the Vocabulary builder and New expressions, i.e. from this unit on you will see **yiruuH** rather than **yi-rúuH**.

Hiwáar 1 *Conversation 1*

08.03 *Ahmed, a Saudi student in Riyadh, is travelling to visit his parents, who live in Doha. He doesn't want to fly, so he goes to the bus station to ask about the bus service to Doha. First listen, then answer the question.*

1 Does Ahmed want a single or return ticket?

Ahmed	fiih baaS yiruuH ad-dooHah min faDH-lak?
kaatib	aywa, fiih baaS yiruuH mubaasharatan.
Ahmed	at-tadhkarah bi-kam?
kaatib	dhihaab bass aw dhiháab w iyáab?
Ahmed	dhiháab w iyáab.
kaatib	miyyah wa khamsah wa :ishriin riyaal.
Ahmed	al-baaS yiTla: as-saa:ah kam?
kaatib	yiTla: as-saa:ah thamaanyah aS-SubaH bi DH-DHabt.
Ahmed	zain, wa mata yooSal ad-dooHah?
kaatib	yooSal as-saa:ah sab:ah wa nuSS al-misa.
Ahmed	nzain. a:Tiini tadhkarat dhiháab w iyáab Hagg baakir. mumkin adfa: bi l-kart?
kaatib	aywa, mumkin.

08.03 **Listen again, and this time speak the part of Ahmed.**

> **PRONUNCIATION TIP**
> The word **zain** (*good, fine*) is sometimes pronounced with an **n**-sound in front of it to make **nzain**.

2 True or false?
  a The ticket costs 120 riyals.
  b The bus leaves at 8 o'clock in the evening.
  c He wants a ticket for tomorrow.

3 Find the Arabic expressions that mean:
  a There is a bus that goes direct.
  b How much is the ticket?
  c What time does the bus leave?
  d When does it arrive in Dubai?
  e Give me a return ticket for tomorrow.

Language discovery

How do you say the following in Arabic?

a *Give me a return ticket?*

b *Is there a bus which goes to Dubai, please?*

> **TIP**
>
> The expression *Give me* ... used when asking for something might seem a little rude or abrupt in English, but this is not the case in Arabic.

1 POSSESSIVE PHRASES

You have already learned the possessive suffixes **-i**, **-ak**, **-ich**, etc. to express the idea of belonging, such as **aish ism-ak?** *What's your name?* (to a man).

You can also express belonging in Arabic by placing two nouns together, the second one usually having **al-** (*the*) in front of it. Here are some possessive phrases you have already come across.

ragam at-tilifoon	*phone number* (lit. *number of the phone*)
sawwaag at-taaksi	*taxi driver* (lit. *driver of the taxi*)
mawgif al-baaS	*bus stop* (lit. *stop of the bus*)
wasaT al-madiinah	*town centre* (lit. *centre of the town*)
suug as-samak	*fish market* (lit. *market of the fish*)

Note that if a feminine noun ending in **-ah** is used as the first part of such a construction it changes to **-at**, as in **tadhkarat dhiháab w iyáab** (*a return ticket*).

madiinat al-kuwait	*Kuwait City* (lit. *city of (the) Kuwait*)
sayyaarat al-mudiir	*the manager's car* (lit. *car of the manager*)
saa:at al-jaami:ah	*the university clock*

In the first word in this construction, never place **al-** in front of it. Instead, always place **al-** in front of the second word.

The indefinite equivalent of such possessive phrases can be seen in the following example.

sawwaag taaksi	*a taxi driver*

2 PLURALS – TALKING ABOUT MORE THAN TWO THINGS

You will have noticed that some nouns in the Vocabulary builder in this unit have something in brackets after them, e.g. **sayyaarah (-aat)** and **tadhkarah (tadhaakir)**. For most words ending in **-ah**, which are usually but not always feminine in gender, you often form the plural by removing the **-ah** and adding **-aat**. But some words, like **tádhkarah**, change their internal shape, e.g. **tadháakir**. Plurals are explained in further detail in *Complete Spoken Arabic* and *Complete Arabic*. For now, you need only learn the plural form with the noun and notice the different forms as you come across them in the Core vocabulary. And remember to use the special dual form for two of anything, as explained in Unit 5.

PRACTICE 1

1 Match the Arabic to the correct English translation.

a	tadhkarat dhiháab w iyáab	**1**	there's no train to Kuwait
b	fiih baaS yiruuH mubaasharatan	**2**	How much is a single ticket?
c	yooSal as-saa:ah thintain	**3**	a return ticket
d	maa fiih giTaar yiruuH al-kuwait	**4**	it arrives at two o'clock
e	tadhkarat dhihaab bass bikam?	**5**	there's a direct bus

2 Complete each sentence by adding the correct word from the box.

> iyáab   mubaasharatan   mata   Hagg
> yiruuH   bi-kam   yiTla: as-saa:ah

a fiih baaS _____ ad-dooHah min faDHlak?

b maa fiih baaS yiruuH _____.

c at-tadhkarah _____?

d dhihaab bass aw dhiháab w _____?

e al-baaS _____ as-saa:ah kam?

f wa _____ yoosal dubáy?

g yooSal _____ sab:ah wa nuSS fi l-misa.

h a:Tiini tadhkarat dhihaab w iyaab _____ baakir.

3 Look at the Muscat to Dubai bus timetable, then say if the following statements are true (T) or false (F).

Buses from Muscat to Dubai		
Muscat International Airport		0625
Muscat, Al Athaiba	dep	0630
Al Musanah		0745
Al Suwaiq	dep	0805
Sohar – Shell Station	dep	0900
Wajajah – border post	arr	1215
Dubai – Abu Hail Station	arr	1240

a yiTla: min masqaT as-saa:ah síttah wa nuSS.
b yooSal fii SoHaar as-saa:ah :asharah wa thilth.
c al-baaS yiruuH mubaasharatan.
d yooSal fii dubáy as-saa:ah :waaHidah illa thilth.

4 Match the Arabic to its English translation.

    a mool al-imaaraat   **1** gold market
    b mawaagif as-sayyaaraat   **2** shopping center
    c markaz tijaari   **3** Sharjah University
    d jaami:at ash-shaarjah   **4** Mall of the Emirates
    e suug adh-dhahab   **5** car park

Listen and understand

1 08.04 **What type of ticket does each traveller want? Listen and select the correct ticket type.**
    a one-way/return ticket
    b one-way/return ticket
    c one-way/return ticket
    d one-way/return ticket

2 Ask if there is a bus to the following destinations.
  a Abu Dhabi
  b Muscat
  c Riyadh
  d Salalah

3 You want to take a train from Dammam to Riyadh. Speak your part of the conversation, following the prompts. You begin.

ínta	*Say good morning.*
Ticket seller	SabaaH an-nuur.
ínta	*Ask if there is a train to Riyadh tomorrow afternoon.*
Ticket seller	na:am, fiih giTaar yiruuH mubaasharatan.
ínta	*Ask what time it leaves.*
Ticket seller	yiTla: as-saa:ah thintain ba:d aDH-DHuhr.
ínta	*Ask what time it arrives in Riyadh.*
Ticket seller	yooSal as-saa:ah waaHidah fi l-lail.
ínta	*Ask how much a return ticket costs.*
Ticket seller	miyyah wa thalaathiin riyaal.

NEW EXPRESSIONS

08.05 Listen and repeat the phrases, then add the missing English words.

a-ríid astá'jir sayyáarah	*I'd like to hire a car.*
a-ríid astá'jir foor-wiil	*I'd like to hire a _____car.*
fii-ha ai-sii?	*Does it have A/C?*
li-múddat aish?	*For how long?*
kam al-iijáar fi l-yoom?	*How much is the rental per day?*
kam al-iijáar li-...	*How much is the rental for ...*
... yoom wáaHid/yoomáin/usbúu:?	*... a _____/two _____/a week?*
si:r makhSúuS	*special price*
tfáDHDHal al-láisan máal-i	*Here's my driving licence.*
háadha s-sí:r má:a t-ta'míin?	*Does this price include insurance?*
as-sáa:ah kam láazim arajjí:-ha?	*What time must I return it?*

Hiwáar 2 *Conversation 2*

08.06 *Louis is in Sharjah and decides to rent a car for the weekend. He arrives at the rental office and speaks to the clerk. First listen, then answer the question.*

1 What kind of car does Louis want to rent?

Louis	ariid asta'jir sayyaarah foor-wiil min faDHlak.
káatib	:ind-na toyoota praado jadiidah. hiyya sayyaarah waajid jamiilah!
Louis	fii-ha ai-sii?
káatib	Tab:an!
Louis	kam al-iijaar fi l-yoom?
káatib	dagiigah min faDHlak ... al-iijaar thalaath miyyah dirham fi l-yoom. tiriid-ha li-muddat aish?
Louis	li-yoomain.
káatib	zain. a:Tiik si:r makhSuuS. khams miyyah wa khamsiin dirham bass.
Louis	haadha s-si:r ma:a t-ta'miin?
káatib	dagiigah min faDHlak ... na:am as-si:r ma:a t-ta'miin.

(*Louis hands over his driver's licence.*)

Louis	tfaDHDHal al-laisan maal-i. as-saa:ah kam laazim arajji:-ha?
káatib	yoom as-sabt, nafs al-wagt ... ya:ani ... as-saa:ah arba:ah.
Louis	tamaam, in sha'Allaah.

(*Later on, Louis stops at a garage for petrol and asks for an oil-check.*)

Louis	a:Tiini :ishriin laitir mumtaaz min faDHl-ak wa mumkin ti-chayyik al-aayil?

> **TIP**
> The term *four-wheel drive car*, or *4x4*, can be expressed either as **foor-wiil** (*four-wheel*), or as **sayyaarah fii-ha dábal**.

2 Answer these questions.
   a How does the clerk describe the car he is suggesting?
   b What does he want to know about the car?
   c How many days does Louis want the car for?
   d How much is the rental for one day?
   e Does the price include insurance?
   f Which day and at what time must he return the car?

3 What is the Arabic for the following?
 a It's a very nice car!
 b One minute, please.
 c Saturday, at the same time.
 d When must I return it?

Language discovery

Find the Arabic expressions that mean:
 a twenty litres of premium
 b Can you check the oil?

LOAN WORDS DERIVED FROM ENGLISH

Gulf Arabic has adopted many words (mainly technical) from English. The plural of these words is usually formed by adding **-áat**, as shown in the brackets. Be aware that this does not apply to Arabic spoken outside the Gulf, for example in Iraq or Egypt.

taayráat jadíidah *new tyres*

An unusual feature of Arabic grammar is that the feminine singular form of adjectives, in this case **jadiidah** (*new*), is used with non-human plural nouns.

Here are some more useful words you might need when driving in the Gulf.

ai-sii	*air-conditioning*
bánchar	*puncture*
biráik	*brakes*
lait (-áat)	*light (of a car)*
taayr (-áat)	*tyre(s)*
wárshah	*workshop*
banzíin	*petrol*
maHáTTat banzíin	*petrol station*
:áadi	*ordinary, regular (petrol)*
mumtáaz	*super, premium (petrol)*
láitir, lítir (-áat)	*litre*
dáizil	*diesel*
kharbáan (adj)	*broken down*

PRACTICE 2

Match the English to the Arabic.

    a I'd like 25 litres of regular, please.   **1** as-sayyaarah maal-ti kharbaanah

    b How much is a litre?   **2** mumkin tichayyik at-taayraat?

    c Can you check the tyres?   **3** laitir bikam?

    d Is there a workshop near here?   **4** ariid khamsah w :ishriin laitir :aadi min faDHlak.

    e My car has broken down.   **5** fiih warshah gariibah min hina?

Go further

READING ARABIC

Both **f** ف (**faa'**) and **q** ق (**qaaf**) look identical at the start and in the middle of a word, but **qaaf** on its own and at the end of a word has a looped tail below the line. Both have dots, one and two respectively. Note that **k** ك (**kaaf**) appears differently in every position.

> **PRONUNCIATION TIP**
> Remember – the letter **q** (**qaaf**) is often pronounced as **g** in Gulf Arabic, so words such as **gahwah** and **gariib** are actually written with a **q** in Arabic script.

end of a word	middle of a word	start of a word	on its own
كيف؟ **kaif?** *how?*	أدفع **a-dfa:** *I pay*	فندق **funduq** *hotel*	ف **faa'**
صديق **Sadiiq** *friend*	دقيقة **daqiiqah** *minute*	قارب **qaarib** *boat*	ق **qaaf**
بنك **bank** *bank*	سكر **sukkar** *sugar*	كيلومتر **kiluumitir** *kilometre*	ك **kaaf**

Look again at this Dubai road sign. Find the **qaaf** in the Arabic word for the place name **Al Quoz**, and the **faa'** in the word **Al Safa**.

Identify the sign that says:

   a mawaaqif as-siinima (*cinema parking*)
   b Burj Khalifah
   c biduun sukkar (*sugar-free*)
   d saykil bark (*cycle park*)

> **PRONUNCIATION TIP**
> As there is no letter *p* in Arabic, foreign words translated into Arabic script usually use the letter **baa'** instead, so *park* becomes **bark**. Likewise, **f** is used instead of *v*, so *video* becomes **fiidiyoo**.

Test yourself

How would you say these phrases in Arabic? The first word has been given to remind you how each phrase starts.

a Is there a bus which goes to Abu Dhabi? **fiih** _____?

b When does it arrive? **mata** _____?

c How much is a single ticket? **tadhkarat** _____?

d Give me a return ticket, please. **a:Tiini** _____

e I want to hire a car, please. **ariid** _____

f How much is the rental for one week? **kam** _____?

g Can I pay by card? **mumkin** _____?

SELF CHECK

I CAN ...
... book and buy travel tickets.
... hire a car.
... buy petrol and deal with basic car problems.

9

In this unit you will learn how to:
» talk about what you do in your free time.
» say what you will do and when.
» say how often you do things.
» make arrangements to meet people.

aish tiHíbb tisáwwi?

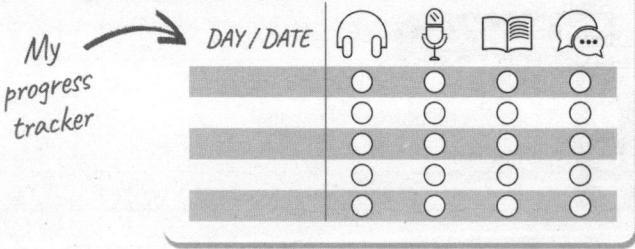

My progress tracker

DAY / DATE	🎧	🎤	📖	💬
	○	○	○	○
	○	○	○	○
	○	○	○	○
	○	○	○	○
	○	○	○	○

Leisure

You are sure to find lots of ways to spend your **wagt al-faráagh** (*free time*) in the Arabian Peninsula. Contrary to popular belief, it's not all **rimáal** (*sand dunes*), although there certainly are plenty of those! Weekends can be filled with water sports such as **as-sibáaHah** (*swimming*) or **al-ghooS** (*diving*). Walking in the **jibáal** (*mountains*) or along a **wáadi** (*valley* or *dry river bed*) is also popular and you are very likely to see families having a **jálsah** (*sitting together, perhaps with a picnic*).

When it comes to **ar-riyáaDhah** (*sport*), **kúrah** (*soccer/football*) is especially popular, and many groups of friends play games at the beach **:ála l-báHar**. If you have a **foor-wiil**, the desert is a great place for **at-takhíyyim** (*camping*) with **al-aSdigáa'** (*friends*). Dune-bashing across the huge, rolling **rimáal** is a favourite pastime, but if you prefer to escape the heat for a while there is always plenty to do at the mall – **at-tasáwwag** (*shopping*), **as-síinima**. In Dubai you can even try **at-tazálluj** (*skiing*)!

Someone asks you, **tiHibb al-kurah?** What are they asking you?

Vocabulary builder

09.01 **First look at these words and phrases, then complete them by adding the missing English words. Now listen and repeat.**

waqt (waqt) al-faráagh	*free time*
Sayd as-sámak	*fishing*
ar-riyáaDHah	*sport*
al-musíiga	_____
as-sibáaHah	*swimming*
al-ghooS	*diving*
at-takhyiim	*camping*
ál:ab ...	*I play ...*
... kúrah	*... soccer/football*
... tánis	*... tennis*
... skwaash	*... _____*
arúuH ...	*I go (to) ...*
... as-suug	*... shopping*
... al-jábal (jibáal)	*... the mountain(s)*
... al-wáadi	*... the wadi (a usually dry valley or river bed)*
... aS-SaHaráa'	*... the desert*
... al-báH(a)r	*... the sea (also beach)*
... as-síinima	*... the _____*
asáwwi ...	*I do, make*
... ríHlah	*... a trip*
... jálsah	*... a gathering*
ashúuf at-tilifizyóon	*I watch _____*
astámi: li l-musíiga	*I listen to music*
ágra (áqra)	*I read*
azúur aSdigáa'	*I visit friends (m)*
azúur Sadiigáat	*I visit friends (f)*

> **TIP**
>
> A **jálsah**, in the social sense, is a general term for a gathering with friends or family and can take the form of a picnic, a barbecue or just sitting around together somewhere pleasant such as a **jálsah :ala l-baHar, :ala l-waadi** or **:ala l-jabal**.

NEW EXPRESSIONS

09.02 Listen to these expressions, then say them out loud.

wain tirúuH?	*Where are you going?*
tiríid tíiji má:na?	*Do you want to come with us?*
maa ál:ab kúrah ábadan	*I never play _____*
aish ti-Híbb ti-sáwwi ...	*What do you like to do ...*
... fii wagt al-faráagh?	*... in your free time?*
aHyáanan ál:ab skwaash	*I sometimes play squash*
ba:d ash-shúghul (*or* ad-dawáam)	*after work*
níjlis fi l-bait.	*We stay/are staying (lit. sitting) at home.*
fi l-bait	*at home*
laish maa nsáwwii ríHla li ...?	*Why don't we make a trip to ...?*
fíkrah wáajid Hílwah	*Great idea!*

Hiwáar 1 *Conversation 1*

09.03 *Sultan and Karim are work colleagues chatting about what they do in their free time. First listen, then answer the question.*

1 Which sport does Karim like playing?

Sultan	ahlan ya kariim, kaif Haalak?
Karim	ahlan ya sulTaan, al-Hamdu li-l-laah. w inta?
Sultan	al-Hamdu li-l-laah. wain tiruuH?
Karim	aruuH al:ab kurah ma:a aSdigaa'-i. nal:ab marrtain fi l-usbuu: :ala l-baHar. tiriid tiiji ma:a?
Sultan	laa, shukran – maa aHibb al-kurah.
Karim	aish tiHibb tisawwi fii wagt al-faraagh?
Sultan	aHyaanan al:ab skwaash ba:d ash-shughul.

(They go on to talk about their plans for the weekend.)

Karim	aish bitsawwi yoom al-khamiis?
Sultan	maa a:raf ... mumkin binijlis fi l-bait, nshuuf at-tilifizyoon.
Karim	laish maa nsawwi riHlah li Suur ma:a al-awlaad?
Sultan	fikrah waajid Hilwah mumkin nsawwi jalsah :ala baHar.
Karim	Tayyib, nruuH yoom al-khamiis fi S-SubaH, ya:ani ... as-saa:ah tis:ah?
Sultan	tamáam, bashuufak yoom al-khamiis as-saa:ah tis:ah, in shaa' Allaah.

09.03 **Listen again and this time speak Karim's part.**

2 What is the correct answer?

    a Karim plays soccer ...

        1 once a week   2 twice a week   3 three times a week

    b Sultan plays squash ...

        1 on Saturday   2 before work   3 after work

    c They are planning a trip to ...

        1 the beach   2 the cinema   3 the mall

3 Match the English to the Arabic.

    a Maybe we'll stay at home.   **1** bashuufak yoom al-khamíis.

    b Great idea.   **2** aruuH al:ab kurah.

    c I'll see you Thursday.   **3** tiriid tiiji ma:na?

    d I'm going to play soccer.   **4** mumkin nijlis fi l-bait.

    e Do you want to come with us?   **5** fikrah waajid Hilwah.

4 Are these statements true (T) or false (F)?

    a Karim plays soccer with his brother.

    b Sultan also likes soccer.

    c They are going to take the children on the trip.

    d They are planning to go on Friday.

Language discovery

What is the Arabic for the words in bold?

    a I play **twice a week**.   **d** Maybe **we will stay at home**.

    b **Sometimes** I play squash.   **e** **I will see you** on Thursday.

    c **I'm going to play** soccer.

1 SAYING HOW OFTEN YOU DO THINGS

 09.04 Here are some phrases you will find useful.

aHyáanan	*sometimes*
dáayman	*always*
kill *or* **kull yoom**	*every day*
márrah/marr(a)táin ...	*once/twice ...*
thaláath marráat ...	*three times ...*
... fi l-yoom	*... a day*
... fi l-usbúu:	*... a week*
... fi sh-sháhar	*... a month*
... fi s-sánah	*... a year*

al-Hiin door-ak! *Now your turn!*

Complete each sentence by adding the correct Arabic.

a _____al:ab tanis. *I sometimes play tennis.*

b aruuH al-mool_____yoom. *I go to the mall every day.*

c al:ab kurah_____fi l-usbuu:. *I play soccer once a week.*

d _____anaam ba:d al-ghada'. *I always sleep after lunch.*

e daayman amshi _____al-:ásha. *I always walk after dinner.*

OMANI SAYING

In Oman there is a helpful saying: **tghádda w tsádda, t:áshsha w tmáshsha**, which translates as *Have lunch, then sleep, have dinner, then walk.*

ABADAN

Use the negative adverb **abadan** in conjunction with **maa** (*not*).

maa arúuH al-mool ábadan. *I never go to the mall.*

If you want to really emphasize *never*, lengthen the last **a** on **abadan**:

maa arúuH al-baHar abadáan! *I <u>never</u> go to the sea!*

---

2 SAYING WHAT YOU WILL DO IN THE FUTURE

Spoken Arabic in the Gulf expresses the future by adding the letter **b-** to the present tense form of the verb. A helping vowel, usually **-i**, is added before a consonant. The vowels of the present tense prefixes are left out to smooth the pronunciation.

barúuH	I will go	binrúuH	we will go
bitrúuH	you (m) will go	bitruuHúun	you (pl) will go
bitruuHíin	you (f) will go		
biyrúuH	he will go	biyruuHúun	they will go
bitrúuH	she will go		

PRACTICE 1

1 Match these sports to the correct Arabic word.

   a booling   **d** at-tazalluj :ala l-maay   **g** Sayd as-samak

   b airoobik   **e** ghooS   **h** goolf

   c kurah   **f** at-tazalluj :ala th-thalj   **i** tanis aT-Taawilah

2 Match the English to the Arabic. Then cover up the Arabic and say the phrases out loud.

a	sometimes	**1**	maa ... abadan
b	always	**2**	marrah fi l-usbuu:
c	never	**3**	aHyaanan
d	once a week	**4**	ba:d al-ghada'
e	every day	**5**	daayman
f	after lunch	**6**	kull yoom

3 Match the Arabic and English forms of the future verb *will go*.

a	you (f) will go	**1**	baruuH
b	we will go	**2**	biyruuH
c	she will go	**3**	bitruuHiin
d	he will go	**4**	binruuH
e	I will go	**5**	bitruuH

4 Match the English to the Arabic, then select the correct future verb form.

a	She will go to Riyadh on Friday.	**1**	basawwi/binsawwi jalsah :ala l-baHar.
b	He will go to the mall after work.	**2**	bashuuf/binshuuf at-tilifizyoon ba:d aDH-DHuhr.
c	I will watch TV in the afternoon.	**3**	biyruuH/bitruuH al-mool ba:d ash-shughal.
d	We will have a BBQ on the beach.	**4**	baruuH/bitruuH ar-riyaaDH yoom al-jum:ah.

Listen and understand

1 09.05 Listen to each speaker talk about their leisure time, then fill in the table with what activity each person does and when or how often they do it.

	Activity?	When/How often?
a		
b		
c		
d		
e		

2 09.06 Salim is interviewing Fatima about what she likes to do in her free time. Which of the ten expressions listed do you hear as they talk? Listen to the conversation as many times as you need.

sometimes	I read	with my friends
sport	cinema	I don't like
music	shopping	
inshaa'Allaah	swimming	

> **TIP**
> fiilm (pl afláam)   *movie*
> waajid   *a lot, much*
> áiDHan   *also*

3 Match each question to its correct answer.

a aish tisawwi fii wagt al-faraagh? **1** na:am, al:ab kurah kull yoom.
b aish tiriid tisawwi yoom **2** ya:ani ... marrtain fi sh-shahar.
 al-khamiis? **3** baruuH al-baHar in shaa'
c tiHibb ar-riyaaDHah? Allaah.
d tiruuH as-siinima waajid? **4** ariid aruuH al-maT:am.
e wain bitruuH yoom al-sabt? **5** al:ab tanis wa skwaash.

4 How would you answer the questions in the previous exercise yourself?

NEW EXPRESSIONS

09.07 Add the missing English words to complete the phrases, then listen and repeat.

báachir/báakir/búkrah	*tomorrow*
mashghúul/mashghúulah	*busy (m/f)*
fáaDHi/fáaDHiyah	*free*
aish al-barnáamij?	*What's the plan (of activity)?*
ayy makáan	*anywhere*
aish rá'y-ak?	*What do you (m) think?*
aish rá'y-ich?	*What _____? (f)*

áasif/áasifah	(I'm) sorry (m/f)
ba:d báakir	(the day) after _____
múmkin nruuH nzuur ...	We could go and visit ...
munáasib/munáasibah	suitable, convenient (m/f)
as-sáa:ah khámsah munáasibah l-ich?	Is five o'clock convenient for you? (f)

al-Hiin door-ak! *Now your turn!*

Ask your brother if it would be convenient for him to meet you at five o'clock.

Hiwáar 2 *Conversation 2*

 09.08 *Fatima is talking to her friend Samira on the phone about what to do on their day off. First listen, then answer the question.*

1 Where do Fatima and Samira decide to go?

Fatima	inti mashghuulah baakir?
Samira	laa, ana faaDHiyah. aish al-barnaamij?
Fatima	maa a:raf. wain tiriidiin tiruuHiin?
Samira	ayy makaan ... aish ra'y-ich?
Fatima	tiriidiin tiruuHiin al-mool?
Samira	laa aasifah, baruuH ba:d baakir in shaa'Allaah ma:a ukhti.
Fatima	mumkin nruuH nzuur salma wa shamsah?
Samira	tamaam. nruuH as-saa:ah kam?
Fatima	as-saa:ah a:sharah munaasibah l-ich?
Samira	aywa. ashuuf-ich baakir in shaa'Allaah.
Fatima	in shaa'Allaah.

2 Answer the following questions.
  a What does Fatima first suggest?
  b Why doesn't Samira want to go?
  c Where do they decide to go?
  d What time do they decide to go?

Language discovery

Find the expressions in the conversation that mean:

a Where do you want to go?

b Do you want to go to the mall?

c We could go and visit Salma and Shamsa.

VERB STRINGS (*I'M GOING TO …* + VERB)

In English we can express future plans or intention by saying *I'm going to* + another verb, as in *I'm going to talk to him tomorrow*. But Arabic doesn't have an infinitive form, so you just keep adding the same form of the verb to your string.

aish tiruuHti sawwi?	*What are you going to do?* (lit. *What you-go you-do?*)
aruuH ashuuf (fiilm).	*I'm going to see (a movie).*
aruuH azuur	*I'm going to visit* (lit. *I-go I-visit*)
aruuH al:ab	*I'm going to play* (lit. *I-go I-play*)
aruuH at:allam	*I'm going to learn* (lit. *I-go I-learn*)
aruuH asawwi	*I'm going to do/make* (lit. *I-go I-do/make*)

PRACTICE 2

1 Rearrange the Arabic to make the sentences given in English. Then say the sentences out loud.

a s-siinima   ashuuf   fi   fiilm   aruuH
I'm going to see a movie in the cinema.

b amshi   l-baHar   aruuH   :ala
I'm going to walk on the beach.

c sidaab   aruuH   ahl-i   azuur   fii
I'm going to visit my family in Sidab.

d aruuH   Sadiig-i   al:ab   ma:a   goolf
I'm going to play golf with my friend.

e agra'   fi   aruuH   l-Hadiigah
I'm going to read in the garden.

f al-lughah   at:allam   al-yabaaniyyah   aruuH
I'm going to learn Japanese.

2 How would you answer these questions yourself?

aish tiruuH tisawwi ...

a baakir?

b yoom as-sabt?

c al-usbuu: al-gaadim (*next week*)?

Go further

 READING ARABIC

In this section you will learn how to read the letters **l** ل (**laam**), **m** م (**miim**), **h** ه (**haa'**) and **w** و (**waaw**). You have already met **laam** in Unit 1 when you learned **alif-laam**, but it is useful to know how it appears in different positions. **miim** is a ball and looks very similar in all its positions. **haa'** looks quite different in each position – try to learn each one. **waaw** looks exactly the same in each position but doesn't join to any letter after it.

end of a word	middle of a word	start of a word	on its own
جبل	رحلة	ليمون	ل
jabal	**riHlah**	**laimoon**	**laam**
mountain	*trip*	*lemon*	
كم	خمسة	مول	م
kam?	**khamsah**	**mool**	**miim**
how much?	*five*	*mall*	
وجه	قهوة	هذا	ه
wajh	**qahwah**	**haadha**	**haa'**
face	*coffee*	*this* (m)	
راديو	غوص	وادي	و
raadyo	**ghooS**	**waadi**	**waaw**
radio	*diving*	*riverbed/ valley*	

1 The letters **laam**, **miim**, **haa'** and **waaw** appear on each of these common signs and labels. Using the table, identify which of these letters appear in each word. Some letters appear more than once in the same word!

Example: a laam and ...

a السوق

b مكتب

c دبي مول

d ممتاز

e حليب

f دورات المياه

2 09.09 Now match up each Arabic sign in exercise 1 to its pronunciation.

> Haliib   dawraat al-miyaah (*bathrooms*)
> dubáy mool   as-suug   máktab (*office*)   mumtaaz (*super*)

3 09.09 Listen to the pronunciation of each word then repeat.

Test yourself

1 In Arabic tell a friend whether you like or dislike these activities.
- **a** scuba diving
- **b** sport
- **c** swimming
- **d** camping

2 Put each sentence into the future tense.
- **a** ana al:ab kurah.
- **b** niHna nal:ab skwaash.
- **c** inta tishuuf at-tilifizyoon.
- **d** huwwa yiruuH al-mool.

3 Say when or how often you participate in each activity. You could use the phrases in the box, or any others you have learned.

> aHyaanan   maa ... abadan   kull yoom
> marrtain fi l-usbuu: marrah fi s-sanah   yoom al-jum:ah

- **a** play tennis
- **b** go to the cinema
- **c** go to the beach
- **d** watch a movie
- **e** visit friends
- **f** listen to music

4 Following the prompts, speak your part in the conversation with Faris.

Faris	inta mashghoul baakir?
inta	*Say no, you're free.*
Faris	aish al-barnaamij
inta	*We could play soccer on the beach.*
Faris	nzain. as-saa:ah kam nruuH?
inta	*Say five o'clock.*
Faris	nzain.
inta	*Say you will hopefully see him tomorrow.*
Faris	in shaa' Allaah. ma:a as-salaamah.
inta	*Say goodbye.*

SELF CHECK

	I CAN ...
○	... talk about what I do in my free time.
○	... say what I will do.
○	... say how often I do things.
○	... make arrangements to meet people.

10

In this unit you will learn how to:
» say the months of the year.
» talk about your last holiday.
» say what you have done.
» describe the weather.

li-wain ruHt fi l-ijáazah?

My progress tracker →

DAY / DATE

Holiday time

Gulf countries observe a number of special Islamic holidays, such as **:iid** (*Eid*) **al-fitr**, a three-day celebration marking the end of the fasting period during Ramadan. At such times roads can get busy and flights and hotels booked up as people make the most of their time off work with friends and family away from home. Of course, weather can be a key factor in deciding when and where to go on holiday. In the Gulf, **al-jaww** (*the weather*) varies from region to region, but in general things can get **wáajid Haarr** (*very hot*) **fi S-Saif** (*in the summer*) and the **dárajat il-Haráarah** (*temperature*) can soar well above 40°C **min máayo li sabtámbar**. Despite the heat, there are countless places to visit during **ijáazat aS-Saif**. You could travel **bi T-Tayyáarah** (*by plane*) to somewhere a little cooler such as the city of Salalah in the south of Oman. During **ash-shíta** (*the winter*), however, temperatures are generally much more pleasant with just a small chance of **máTar** (*rain*) or even **thalj** (*snow*) high up in the **jábal**.

Find the Arabic for:
a from May to September
b the summer holiday
c mountain

Vocabulary builder

10.01 First add the missing English words, then listen and repeat the Arabic out loud.

SHUHÚUR AS-SÁNAH	MONTHS OF THE YEAR
yanáayir	January
fibráayir	February
mars	March
abríil	_____
máayo	May
yúunyo	June
yúulyo	July
aghúsTos	_____
sabtámbar	September
októobar	October
nufámbar	November
disámbar	_____
fii yanáayir	in January
fii abríil	in April
fi S-Saif	in the summer
fi sh-shíta	in the winter

NEW EXPRESSIONS

10.02 Add the missing English words, then listen and repeat the Arabic out loud.

as-sánah l-máaDHiyah	last _____
ruHt hináak min gábil?	Have you (m) been there before?
kaan	was (m)
káanat	was (f)
áwwal márrah	the _____ time
áwwalan	firstly, first of all
sáafart	I travelled
sáafarna	_____ travelled
ruHt	I went
rúHna	we went
zurt	_____ visited
zúrna	we visited
kaif sáafartu?	How did you (pl) travel?

bi T-Tayyáarah	by _____
bi s-sayyáarah	by _____
aish sawwáitu?	What did you (pl) do?
sawwáina ríHlah	we went on a trip (lit. we made a trip)
shuft Huut	_____ saw a whale
shúfna Huut	we saw a whale
ishtaráit	I bought
ishtaráina	_____ bought
min sanatáin	two years ago
waalidáin	parents
biláad (f) (buldáan pl)	country
sámak (pl. asmáak)	fish
ashyáa' kathíirah	many things
mumtáaz/mumtáazah	excellent

Hiwáar 1 *Conversation 1*

10.03 *Saif asks Oliver about where he went on his last holiday. First listen, then answer the question.*

1 Which two countries did Oliver visit?

Saif	li-wain ruHtu fi l-ijaazah?
Oliver	as-sanah l-maaDHiyah ruHt al-imaaraat w :umaan ma:a waalidaini.
Saif	:umaan bilaad waajid jamiilah. ruHt hinaak min gabil?
Oliver	laa, kaanat haadhi awwal marrah. inta ta:raf :umaan?
Saif	na:am. ruHt hinaak min sanatain. kaif saafartu?
Oliver	awwalan saafarna min landan li-dubáy bi T-Tayyaarah wa ba:dain ruHna masqaT bi s-sayyaarah. kaanat riHlah waajid Tawiilah laakin masqaT madiinah jamiilah.
Saif	aish sawwaitu fii masqaT?
Oliver	zurna suug as-samak wa suug adh-dhahab. sawwaina riHlah li l-baHar w shufna Huut w asmaak kathiirah.
Saif	w aish sawwaitu fi l-imaaraat?
Oliver	zurna mataaHif kathiirah fi sh-sharjah wa shufna burj khaliifah fii dubáy. fii aakhir yoom zurt al-mool w ishtarait ashyaa' kathiirah. kaanat ijaazah mumtaazah.
Saif	maa shaa' Allaah!

Listen again, and this time speak the part of Oliver.

> **BEWARE THE WADI!**
> Rainy days are few and far between in most parts of the Gulf, so when it rains, it is quite an event! As the ground is usually so dry, a **wadi** can fill up very quickly and become dangerous to cross, so be careful or you might find yourself stranded on one side for several hours!

2 Match the Arabic to the correct English.

a	li-wain ruHt fi l-ijaazah?	**1**	It was a long journey.
b	kaanat riHlah waajid Tawiilah.	**2**	What did you do in the Emirates?
c	zurna suug as-samak.	**3**	I bought many things.
d	aish sawwaitu fi l-imaaraat?	**4**	We visited the fish market.
e	ishtarait ashyaa' kathiirah.	**5**	Where did you go during the holidays?

3 Are these statements true (T) or false (F)?

a Oliver went to Muscat by car.

b They made a trip to the mountains.

c They visited the museum in Muscat.

d On the last day he went to the shopping mall.

10.03 4 Listen to the conversation again, then choose the correct answers.

a When did Oliver go on holiday?

  i last week   **ii** last month

  iii last year   **iv** two years ago

b This was his _____ visit to Oman.

  i first   **ii** second

  iii third   **iv** fourth

c Where <u>didn't</u> they go?

  i to the shops   **ii** to the beach

  iii to the museum   **iv** to the wadi

Language discovery

Say out loud the Arabic for each expression in bold.

a Last year **I went** to Oman.

b **We saw** a whale and a lot of fish.

c **We made** a trip to the beach.

d **I visited** the shopping mall.

With most Arabic verbs the past tense is formed by adding an ending (or suffix) to the past stem. There are no prefixes, only suffixes. There is no word in Arabic like English *to go*; instead, the past tense *he*-form is used, which is the simplest, with no suffix, and this is the past stem.

Many verbs have just one past stem, like **katab** (*he wrote*).

Singular	Meaning	Plural	Meaning
katáb-t	*I wrote*	**katáb-na**	*we wrote*
katáb-t	*you* (m) *wrote*	**katáb-tu**	*you* (pl) *wrote*
katáb-ti	*you* (f) *wrote*		
kátab	*he wrote*	**kátab-u**	*they wrote*
kátab-at	*she wrote*		

1 **Here are the past stems of some more verbs you have learned that follow the same pattern as katab in the past tense.**

Past stem	Meaning
la:ib	*played*
sáafar	*travelled*
rája:	*returned*
takállam	*spoke*
ishtághal	*worked*
sábaH	*swam*
shárab	*drank*

al-Hiin door-ak! *Now your turn!*

   a Put each verb in the table above into the past tense *I*-form, e.g. **la:ibt** *I played*.

   b Put each verb into the past tense *we*-form, e.g. **la:ibna** *we played*.

2 Some verbs have two past stems, such as **ruH/raaH** (*go*). Only the *he-*, *she*- and *they*-forms use the **raaH**-stem. All other forms use the **ruH**-stem.

Singular	Meaning	Plural	Meaning
ruH-t	*I went*	**rúH-na**	*we went*
ruH-t	*you* (m) *went*	**rúH-tu**	*you* (pl) *went*
rúH-ti	*you* (f) *went*		
raaH	*he went*	**ráaH-u**	*they went*
ráaH-at	*she went*		

Here are some common verbs with two past tense stems. In each pair the *he-/she-/they*-stem is given second, as in **ruH/raaH**. The present stem has also been given to help you recognize verbs you have already met in previous units.

Past stem	Present stem	Meaning
ruH/raaH	ruuH	*go*
nam/naam	naam	*sleep*
zur/zaar	zuur	*visit*
shuf/shaaf	shuuf	*see*

There are other verbs with two past stems but which work in a slightly different way, e.g. *do* or *make*.

Past stem	Meaning	Past stem	Meaning
sawwái-t	*I did, made*	sawwái-na	*we did, made*
sawwái-t	*you* (m) *did, made*	sawwái-tu	*you* (pl) *did, made*
sawwái-ti	*you* (f) *did, made*		
sáww-a	*he did, made*	sáww-u	*they did, made*
sáww-at	*she did, made*		

The verbs **ishtara/ishtari** (*buy*), **mashi/masha** (*walk*) and **gara** (*read*) work in the same way.

For more details of the past tense, see *Complete Arabic* and *Complete Spoken Arabic*.

PRACTICE 1

1 Match the Arabic to the correct English.

    a al-usbuu: al-maaDHi   **1** last year

    b ash-shahr al-maaDHi   **2** last week

    c as-sanah al-maaDHiyah   **3** last month

2 Match the Arabic to the correct English.

    a ruHt   **1** I visited

    b sawwait   **2** I drank

    c ishtarait   **3** I went

    d zurt   **4** I did, made

    e shuft   **5** I bought

    f sharabt   **6** I saw

3 Change the present to the past tense, then say each sentence. Begin each sentence with **ams** (*yesterday*).

- **a** ana aruuH as-siinima.
- **b** huwwa yishrab gahwah.
- **c** niHna nizuur al-matHaf.
- **d** inti tiruuHiin al-mool.
- **e** huwwa yishtaghal fi l-máktab.
- **f** humma yiruuHuun suug adh-dhahab.

TIP
Pronouns have been given to help you, but remember that pronouns are optional when speaking Arabic.

4 Now translate your answers from exercise 3 into English.

5 Here is Fatima's message to her friend Samia in Baghdad. Are the following statements true (T), false (F), or not in text (NT)?

:aziizati saamiya,

kaif Haal-ich w aish akhbaar-ich? ash-shahr al-maaDHi ana ruHt al-baHrain ma:a ukhti :azza. zurna qal:at al-baHrain w mool kabiir ismuh 'baHrain siti santar'. hinaak ishtarait kutub kathiirah w ukhti ishtarat malaabis jadidah. aHibb as-safar!

akhi aHmad yiskun fii dubáy wa yizuur abu DHabi waajid. al-usbuu: al-maaDhi zaar jaami: ash-shaikh zaayid al-kabiir ma:a aSdigaa min faransa. al-jaami: waajid jamiil w kabiir! Sadiigati sharloot raaHat dubáy gabil shahr w zaarat Hadiigat al-maaya. inti ruHti dubáy min gabil?

faaTimah ☺

- **a** Fatima visited Bahrain with her brother.
- **b** Fatima bought new clothes.
- **c** Her brother lives in Dubai.
- **d** Her brother is an engineer.
- **e** Fatima visited Sheikh Zayed Grand Mosque.
- **f** Her friend Charlotte visited Dubai last year.
- **g** Her brother visited a water park.

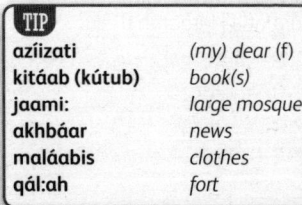

TIP

aziizati	(my) dear (f)
kitáab (kútub)	book(s)
jaami:	large mosque
akhbáar	news
maláabis	clothes
qál:ah	fort

6 Where a statement is false, give the true statement in English.

7 Now imagine that the email was sent to you. Reply in Arabic, saying where you went on your last holiday and giving three activities you did.

8 10.04 What happened on Friday? Listen to each person and list their activities in English.

	morning	afternoon
a		
b		
c		
d		

9 **aish sawwait ams?** *What did you do yesterday?* Complete the phrases with your own activities in the past tense.

  a ams (*yesterday*)
  b al-khamiis al-maaDHi (*last Thursday*)
  c ash-shahar al-maaDHi (*last month*)
  d as-sanah al-maaDHiyah? (*last year*)

NEW EXPRESSIONS

10.05 **Listen, then repeat out loud.**

al-jaww	*the weather*
al-jaww zain	*the weather is good*
al-jaww muu zain	*the weather is not good*
al-jaww báarid (adj)	*the weather is cold*
al-jaww Haarr (adj)	*the weather is hot*
fiih ...	*it's ... [lit. there is]*
... shams	*... sunny (lit. there is sun)*
... ghaim	*... cloudy (lit. there are clouds)*
... háwa	*... windy (lit. there is wind)*
... máTar	*... raining (lit. there is rain)*
... thalj	*... snowing (lit. there is snow)*
dárajat il-Haráarah thalathíin	*it is 30°C (lit. degree the-heat (is) 30)*
móosam aS-Saif	*the season (of) summer*
móosam ash-shíta	*the season (of) winter*

Now cover up the Arabic and repeat out loud.

Instead of **al-jaww báarid/Haarr** you can use:

fiih bard (noun)	*it is cold* (lit. *there is cold*)
fiih Harr (noun)	*it is hot* (lit. *there is heat*)

Hiwáar 2 *Conversation 2*

10.06 Robin is asking Khamis about his business trip to Australia last month.

1 First listen, then answer the questions below.

Robin	kaif kaan al-jaww fii sidni?
Khamis	al-usbuu: al-awwal kaan al-jaww Haarr, laakin al-usbuu: ath-thaani kaan fiih bard w maTar w hawa shwayya.
Robin	ya khasaarah! fii yanaayir?
Khamis	aywa, al-Hiin móosam aS-Saif fii ustraaliya.
Robin	saHiiH.
Khamis	inta ruHt ustraaliya min gabil?
Robin	laa abadan, ustraaliya waajid ba:iidah :an ingilterra! ruHt ayy makaan ghair hinaak?
Khamis	aywa, :indi Sadiig gariib min brizban. ruHt bi T-Tayaarah - brizban ba:iidah :an sidni! kunt fii brisban yoomain bass.

> **TIP**
> **saHiiH** *true*   **khasaarah** *shame, pity*

Match the Arabic to the English.

a	kaan fiih bard w maTar.	**1**	How was the weather?
b	brizban ba:iidah :an sidni.	**2**	It was cold and it rained.
c	ruHt bi T-Tayaarah.	**3**	Did you go anywhere else?
d	kaif kaan al-jaww?	**4**	I went by plane.
e	ruHt ayy makaan ghair?	**5**	Brisbane is far from Sydney.

2 When was Khamis in Sydney?

   a January   **b** April   **c** July

3 How many times has Robin been to Australia?

   a once   **b** twice   **c** never

4 For how long was Khamis in Brisbane?
    a one day   **b** two days   **c** a week

5 Find the Arabic for:
    a The weather was hot.
    b It was cold and it rained.
    c I was in Brisbane for just two days.

Language discovery

1 KAAN

In Arabic no verb is used for *is/are*, but the verb **kaan** means *was/were*. Here is another verb with two past tense stems!

Singular	Meaning	Plural	Meaning
kun-t	*I was*	kún-na	*we were*
kun-t	*you (m) were*	kún-tu	*you (pl) were*
kún-ti	*you (f) were*		
kaan	*he was*	káan-u	*they were*
káan-at	*she was*		

> **TIP**
> **kaan** has a present tense form **yikúun**, but **yikúun** can also imply a future or potential event. For further details, see *Complete Arabic* and *Complete Spoken Arabic*.

NEW EXPRESSIONS

 10.07 Listen and repeat.

kunt fii madiinat al-kuwait as-sabt al-maaDHi.	*I was in Kuwait city last Saturday.*
kaan al-jaww baarid.	*The weather was cold.*
ams kunna fi l-mool.	*Yesterday we were in the mall.*
kaan fiih masbaH fi l-fundug.	*There was a pool in the hotel.*
kaan :indi foor-wiil fii dubáy.	*I had a 4x4 in Dubai.*

> **TIP**
> To make **kaan** negative, just add **maa** before it. For example:
> **maa kaan fiih shams.**   *It wasn't sunny.*
> **maa kaan :indi wagt.**   *I didn't have time.*

al-Hiin door-ak! *Now your turn!*

 Say each sentence out loud in Arabic. Start with the correct form of kaan.

    a I was in Doha last week.

    b The restaurant was closed on Friday.

    c The movie was very good.

    d He had a big house in London.

    e There were a lot of people in the market yesterday.

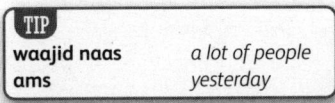

TIP	
waajid naas	*a lot of people*
ams	*yesterday*

2 SAYING HOW THE WEATHER WAS IN THE PAST

To talk about the weather in the past tense, just add **kaan** to the beginning of the phrase.

▶ **al-jaww zain** → **kaan al-jaww zain**

▶ **fiih maTar** → **kaan fiih maTar**

kaan fiih Haar, wa kaanat darajat il-Haraarah arba:iin.
It was hot, and the temperature (f) *was 40°C.*

PRACTICE 2

1 Match the English to the Arabic.

    a The weather is cold.   **1** al-jaww muu zain.

    b It is raining.   **2** fiih thalj.

    c It is hot.   **3** al-jaww baarid.

    d The weather is not good.   **4** al-jaww zain.

    e It is snowing.   **5** fiih Harr.

    f The weather is nice.   **6** fiih maTar.

 2 Now say each Arabic phrase using the past tense.

3 Match the Arabic to the English.

    a kaan   **1** she was

    b kunna   **2** you were (f, sing)

    c kaanat   **3** he was

    d kaanu   **4** we were

    e kunt   **5** they were

    f kunti   **6** I was

Go further

READING ARABIC

Congratulations on reaching Unit 10 of Reading Arabic! You have completed the hardest part by learning all the letters of the Arabic alphabet in their different positions, so now you can begin to read some simple sentences in Arabic.

One of the more challenging aspects of reading Arabic is that usually only the long vowels are shown in the script. Thus, the written word **kitaab** (*book*) would look like **k-t-aa-b**. The **i** sound after the **k** is not written so how can you tell if the letter **k** is pronounced **ka**, **ku**, **ki**, or simply **k**? In this final part of Reading Arabic we introduce you to the short vowels (**a-i-u**), the doubling symbol (**sháddah**) and the zero-vowel symbol (**sukúun**).

SHORT VOWELS, SHÁDDAH AND SUKÚUN

Short vowel symbols are added above and below Arabic letters to help you recognize how to pronounce those letters. Note that in Arabic there is no *e* or *o* vowel.

The short vowel symbols are:

a – a small dash above the letter (known as **fátHah**) as in the **ba**-sound بَ in **bank** (*bank*) بَنك

i – a small dash below the letter (known as **kásrah**) as in the **ki**-sound كِ in **kitáab** (*book*) كِتاب

u – a mini letter **waaw** symbol above the letter (known as **Dámmah**), as in the **du**-sound دُ in **dukkáan** (*shop*) دُكان

Two additional symbols which are useful to recognize to help you read and pronounce a word accurately are:

sháddah, which shows where a letter is doubled. For example, in the word سيّارة **sayyáarah** (*car*), a **sháadah** is placed above the letter **yaa'** يّ to indicate the doubled **yy** sound.

sukúun, which shows that there is no vowel sound at all after the main sound of the letter, as in the **k** ك in مَكتب (*office*).

> **TIP**
> A **shaddah** looks like a little, curvy English letter *w* above the letter that is doubled, and a **sukuun** looks like a little *zero*.

You will have noticed that none of the words introduced in Arabic script so far, including the photos of signs and labels, have shown these symbols.

This is quite normal in Arabic. But many Arabic students' books show them in the Arabic script, so it is very useful to understand what they mean once you begin to advance your Arabic to the next level.

1 In each sentence, identify the Arabic word that matches its English description. Read from right to left.

a	Something to eat?	أنا أحب السمك
b	Something to drink?	أشرب القهوة كل يوم
c	A method of transport?	سافرت إلى دبي بالسيارة
d	A day of the week?	المطعم مفتوح كل يوم سبت

2 What do the words you have identified mean in English?

a _____   c _____

b _____   d _____

3 10.08 Now read out loud each sentence in Arabic written with the short vowels, **shaddah** and **sukuun** marked where appropriate. Remember to read from right to left. Then listen to the speakers to check your pronunciation.

a أَنَا أُحِبُّ السَّمَكَ	
b أَشْرَبُ الْقَهْوَةَ كُلَّ يَوْمٍ	
c سَافَرْتُ إِلَى دُبَي بِالسَّيَارَة	
d الْمَطْعَمْ مَفْتُوحْ كُلَّ يُومْ سبت	

> **PRONUNCIATION**
> Remember that the **laam** in **alif-laam** is not pronounced before a Sun letter!

4 What does each sentence mean in English?

> **TIP**
> As explained in the Introduction, the spoken Arabic you hear and the written Arabic you see may not always use exactly the same form because written Arabic is not usually spoken, and vice versa, but don't worry about this – this is quite usual all over the Arab world and you will get used to it as your Arabic improves. At this stage, whenever you come across Arabic, whether written or spoken, just listen or watch out for key words and phrases you recognize to help you get started.

Mastering the short vowels, and the **shaddah** and **sukuun** symbols will help to accelerate your learning and ability to read Arabic script. It is not easy, but do stick at it – being able to understand Arabic script when you are out and about in the Gulf is one of the most rewarding aspects of learning Arabic.

Develop your Arabic reading and writing skills further with *Complete Arabic*.

Test yourself

 1 Look at the pictures. In Arabic, tell a friend what you did.

a

c

b

d

 2 Answer the questions, telling your friend in Arabic about your last holiday. You may wish to use some of the words/phrases in the box.

ruHt	shuft	ishtarait	kaan
bi s-sayyaarah	ma:a	saafart	zurt

a li-wain ruHt fi l-ijaazah? (*Where did you go on holiday?*)

b ma:a man? (*With whom?*)

c kaif saafart? (*How did you travel?*)

d aish sawwait? (*What did you do?*)

e kaif kaan al-jaww? (*How was the weather?*)

SELF CHECK

I CAN . . .

○	... say the months of the year.
○	... talk about my last holiday.
○	... say what I have done.
○	... describe the weather.

R3

Review: Units 7–10

1 **Match each place in town to its correct name in English.**

a	máaktab bariid	**1**	police station
b	fundug	**2**	hospital
c	mustashfa	**3**	town centre
d	markaz ash-shurTah	**4**	fish market
e	suug as-samak	**5**	hotel
f	wasaT al-madiinah	**6**	post office

2 **What do these people like doing? Read each statement out loud in Arabic, then give your answers in English.**

a **Fatima:** ana aHibb aruuH as-siinima.

b **Ahmed:** ana al:ab kurah.

c **Qaasim:** ana aHibb as-sibaaHah w al-ghooS.

> **TIP**
> **kídha**   *that sort of thing, like that*

d **Faisal:** ana maa aHibb al-kurah, afaDHDHal al:ab skwaash.

e **Laila:** ana aHibb asawwi jalsah aw aruuH as-suug ma:a Sadiigaati.

f **Sara:** ana maa aHibb ar-riyaaDHah. ufadDHil-musiiga, w ijlis fi l-bait, ashuuf al-afláam, kidha …

3 **Ask the way to these places in town. Remember to start with law samaHt or law samaHti (as appropriate).**

a	the beach (to a man)	**d**	the airport (to a man)
b	the market (to a woman)	**e**	the bank (to a man)
c	the pharmacy (to a woman)	**f**	the supermarket (to a woman)

4 **What's the grammar rule here? Complete the sentence by adding the missing Arabic phrases.**

To say *there is/there are* you say _____, and to say *there isn't/there aren't* you say _____.

5 **Match the Arabic to the English, saying the Arabic out loud.**

a	liff yisaar	**1**	take the first right
b	khudhi awwal yamiin	**2**	at the roundabout
c	ruuH siidah	**3**	second right
d	ba:d ad-dawwaar	**4**	turn left
e	thaani yamiin	**5**	after the roundabout
f	:ind ad-dawwaar	**6**	go straight on

6 List the ordinal numbers in order from lowest to highest, saying them out loud in Arabic.

a	thaalith	**d**	thaani	**g**	raabi:
b	taasi:	**e**	khaamis	**h**	saadis
c	saabi:	**f**	thaamin	**i**	awwal

7 Rearrange the Arabic letters to make six words/phrases relating to free time (**wagt al-faraagh**).

a	auhkr	**d**	isimagu
b	hljaas	**e**	nisamii
c	Hashaaib	**f**	Hrau la-lomo

8 Rearrange these Arabic words to make five sentences about **al-jaww**, then say the completed sentences out loud.

    a zain al-yoom al-jaww

    b fi al-jaww l-baHrain kaif?

    c al-jaww baarid kaan

    d maTar aS-SubaH fiih kaan

    e wa il-Haraarah thalaathiin sittah darajat

9 Which is the odd one out in each case?

    a baarid shams thalj falaafil

    b bi T-Tayyaarah bi-sukkar bi s-sayyaarah bi l-baaS

    c azuur asawwi azrag al:ab

    d daayman kull yoom fi s-suug marrah fi l-usbuu:

    e :ala kam foog ba:d

    f sawwaag at-taaksi wasaT al-madiinah
       mawgif al-baaS markaz ash-shurTah

10 Can you complete these grammar rules correctly?

    a To make the future tense, just add _____ to the present tense form of the verb.

    b To say *there was* (instead of *there is*), add _____ (m) or _____ (f) in front of the word **fiih**.

    c To use an imperative to a woman, add _____ to the masculine imperative.

11 Match each Arabic statement to its correct English translation.

a	ista'jarna sayyáarah kabiirah.	**1**	He bought a new coffee pot.
b	saafart ams li d-dooHah.	**2**	The bus went direct.
c	al-baaS raja: min ad-dooHah.	**3**	She swam in the pool.
d	sabaHat fi l-masbaH.	**4**	The bus returned from Doha.
e	ishtara dallah jadiidah.	**5**	I travelled to Doha yesterday.
f	raaH al-baaS mubaasharatan.	**6**	We hired a big car.

12 **Which months are missing here?**

yanaayir   _____

fibraayir   _____

_____   sabtambar

abriil   oktoobar

_____   _____

yuunyo   _____

13 **Read each sentence out loud and state whether the past (P) or future (F) tense is being used.**

  a saafart li-amriika yoom al-aHad.

  b bitruuh al-mool yoom al-khamiis.

  c bashuuf al-fiilm al-jadiid fi s-siinima.

  d ishtaghal fi l-máktab aS-SabaH.

  e aish biysawwi fi S-Saif?

  f sharabna :aSiir fii maT:am.

 AL-KHATT AL-:ARABI *THE ARABIC SCRIPT*

Now that you are more familiar with Arabic script, practice the reading skills you have developed throughout *Beginners' Arabic* by looking at these authentic Arabic signs and answering the following questions.

14 **Read this travel sign and choose the correct option.**

The next bus/boat/train leaves in two minutes.

القطار القادم

2 دقائق

15 **What would you buy here?**
  a medicine   **b** shoes   **c** train tickets

16 **This shop has a sale. But what's the offer?**
  a 10% discount
  b three for the price of two
  c buy one, get one free

17 **This toy shop is having a sale. What discount is available?**
  a 10–20%
  b 20–50%
  c 25–50%

18 You need to report an accident – which of these words says *Police*?

a

b

19 You and a friend are sitting in a café. Your friend does not read Arabic so it's up to you to read the menu and answer your friend's questions (prices are in UAE dirhams).

a How much is a large iced cappuccino?

b How much is a small iced cappuccino 'supreme'?

c Which size smoothie costs 16 dirham?

> **TIP**
> It is worth noting that traditional texts, such as Qur'an, will always use the classical Arabic numerals, so it is still worth learning them; rarely will you see them on a real coffee menu.

المشروبات الباردة

مثلجات

كبير	وسط	صغير	
١٨	١٦	١٤	كابوتشينو مثلج
٢١	١٩	١٧	كابوتشينو مثلج سوبريم
			ما نفضله من النكهات
١٨	١٦	١٤	سموثي بالفواكه الطبيعية

20 Look at the opening days and times for this shopping mall, then decide whether each statement is true (T) or false (F).

a The mall opens at 9 a.m. every day.

b It closes at 10 p.m. Sunday to Wednesday.

c It closes at 11 p.m. on Saturday.

You have now successfully completed *Beginners' Arabic.*

alf mabruuk! *Congratulations!*

Answer key

PRONUNCIATION

Moon letters – a, c, d (al-kháali), f (al-áwsaT), h, j
Sun letters – b, d (ar-rúb:), e, f (ash-sharq), g, i

UNIT 1

The Gulf

(al-)lúghah

Conversation 1

1 morning
2 a no; **b** Dubai
3 a3; **b**4; **c**1; **d**5; **e**2

Language discovery

a there is no Arabic word for *is* or *are*
b ínta is the form used when speaking to a man. **ínti** is the form used when speaking to a woman.
c There are three different endings: **-i**, **-ak**, **-ich** (indicates different people)

Now your turn!

ána ísm-i [your name]

Now your turn!

ána min ustráalya

Practice 1

1 a ísm-i; **b** min; **c** gáTar; **d** Háal-ich
2 -ich; -i; ínta; -ak; -ak; ínti
3 a ísm-i; **b** ísm-ak; **c** ána; **d** ínta; **e** Háal-ich

Listen and understand

1 a5 **b**2 **c**1 **d**6 **e**4 **f**3
2 a m; **b** f; **c** f; **d** m; **e** f; **f** m

Conversation 2

1 Mark: England; Sara: America
2 London
3 a3; **b**4; **c**5; **d**2; **e**1

Language discovery

1 húwwa means *he*; **híyya** means *she*
2 háadha means *this* when referring to a man; **háadhi** means *this* when referring to a woman

Practice 2

1 a húwwa; **b** híyya; **c** híyya; **d** húwwa
2 a háadhi fáaTimah; **b** híyya min ábu DHábi?; **c** laa, híyya min gáTar.
3 a m; **b** m; **c** m; **d** f; **e** f; **f** m
4 a háadha málik, húwwa min másqat; **b** háadha náasir, húwwa min jáddah; **c** háadhi Híbah, híyya min al-yáman; **d** háadhi sofia híyya min isbáanya

Reading Arabic

1 Read the Arabic from right to left.

السُّودان **4**   العِرَاق **3**   الكُّويت **1**

1 Kuwait **2** Iraq **3** Sudan
2 1 as-sudáan; **2** :umáan; **3** al-yáman; **4** al-:iráaq; **5** al-baHráin; **6** qáTar
3 they appear at the beginning of each (reading from right to left)

Test yourself

1 a w :aláikum as-saláam; **b** masáa' an-núur; **c** ísm-i ...; **d** ána min...;
e má:a s-saláamah
2 a :aláikum; **b** wa; **c** min; **d** ána; **e** SabáaH or masáa'; **f** kaif;
g háadhi or ísm-i
3 a aish ísm-ich; **b** aish ísm-ak; **c** kaif Háal-ak

UNIT 2

Arabic numbers

9, 3, 1, 2

Vocabulary builder

1 a5; **b**6; **c**4; **d**2; **e**1; **f**3; **g**7
2 a Arabic; **b** English; **c** Spanish; **d** French

New expressions

Arabic, English, English, English

Conversation 1

1 Emirati

Now your turn!

c hit the brakes immediately
2 a Do you speak English? **b** only Arabic; **c** she speaks it very well; **d** laa;
e Lauren; **f** Alex
3 a F, he speaks Arabic; **b** T; **c** F, he is Emirati

Language discovery

1 Nasser is describing himself so he uses the masculine form, **-i**. Lauren is describing herself so she uses the feminine form, **-íyyah**.
2 a a-takállam; **b** ta-takállam; **c** ta-takallam-íin

Practice 1

1 a m; **b** f; **c** m; **d** f; **e** f; **f** m; **g** m; **h** f; **i** m; **j** f
2 a ingliz-íyyah; **b** ínti iTal-íyyah; **c** híyya :umaan-íyyah; **d** híyya sudaan-íyyah; **e** ána briTaan-íyyah; **f** ínti gaTar-íyyah
3 a I am English, from London. **b** Are you Italian? **c** He is Omani. **d** He is Sudanese. **e** I am British, from Scotland. **f** Are you Qatari?
4 a 2; **b** 3; **c** 1
5 ínta, inglíizi, min, laa, laa, wáajid zain, shwáyya

Listen and understand

2 a 3; **b** 5; **c** 1; **d** 4; **e** 6; **f** 2
3 1 ána amríik-i; 2 ána iskutlánd-i; 3 ána inglíiz-i; 4 ána ustráal-i;
5 ána kuwait-íyyah; 6 ána farans-íyyah

Conversation 2

1 a kam rágam tilifóon-ak? **b** rágam tilifóon-i
2 a T; **b** T; **c** F-521708

Practice 2

1 e, d, b, f, c, a
2 2; 10; 3; 7; 6; 1; 5
4 a zero, seven; **b** Britain, the Emirates; **c** France, Egypt; **d** Ireland, please
5 a Bahraini (f); **b** English (f); **c** Omani (m); **d** Emirati (m); **e** Qatari (f);
f French (m)
6 a 2 Fadia – Yemen; **b** 4 Sausan – Saudi Arabia; **c** 5 Hamdan – Iraq;
d 6 Mohammed – Qatar; **e** 3 Noor – Emirates; **f** 1 Saif – Oman

Reading Arabic

1 a3; **b**5; **c**1; **d**2; **e**4

2 a4; **b**1; **c**5; **d**2; **e**3

Test yourself

1 a inglíiz-i; **b** farans-íyyah; **c** gátar-i; **d** kuwait-íyyah; **e** iskutláand-i;
f baHrain-íyyah; **g** hind-ii; **h** Sin-iyyah

2 a sáb:ah; **b** thaláathah; **c** tís:ah; **d** wáaHid; **e** síttah; **f** ithnáin;
g khámsah; **h** :ásharah

3 a Sífir, khámsah, khámsah – ithnáin, thamáanyah, árba:ah – thaláathah,
wáaHid, thaláathah, árba:ah.

b Sífir, síttah, wáaHid, thamáanyah, thaláathah, sáb:ah, árba:ah, tís:ah,
tís:ah.

c Sífir, árba:ah, sáb:ah, khámsah, wáaHid, síttah, ithnáin, thamáanyah,
wáaHid.

UNIT 3

Getting to know Arabic speakers

coffee, tea

Vocabulary builder

girls/daughters; sisters

New expressions

work

Now your turn!

a-shtághal fii mádrasah

Conversation 1

1 Sally lives in Dubai; no, she does not work

2 a nurse; **b** (big) company in Abu Dhabi; **c** bank

3 a wain ti-skun-íin al-Hiin? **b** ná-skun fii másqaT. **c** ... láakin níHna min
Suur. **d** aish ti-shtaghal-íin? **e** ána mubramij(at) kombuter. **f** ána maa
a-shtághal.

Language discovery

1 níHna, íntu

2 a I work; **b** you work (f); **c** he works

Now your turn!

Arabic – singular	English	Arabic – plural	English
(ána) a-shtághal	I work	(níHna) na-shtághal	we work
(ínta) ti-shtághal	you (m) work	(íntu) ti-shtaghal-úun	you (m/f pl) work
(ínti) ti-shtaghal-íin	you (f) work		
(húwwa) yi-shtághal	he works	(húmma) yi-shtaghal-úun	they (m/f) work
(híyya) ti-shtághal	she works		

Now your turn!

(húwwa) yi-shtághal fii shárikah

Practice 1

1 a húmma; **b** ínti; **c** ána; **d** íntu
2 a yi-shtághal; **b** ti-shtághal; **c** a-shtághal; **d** yi-shtaghal-úun
3 a mudárrisah; **b** Tabíib; **c** mikáaniki; **d** muhándisah
4 ána muhándis wa a-shtághal fii shárikah
6 a f **b** m **c** m **d** f **e** f **f** m
7 a singular; **b** plural; **c** plural; **d** singular

Listen and understand

1 a engineer; **b** doctor; **c** student; **d** teacher; **e** mechanic;
f company director; **g** computer programmer
2 a teacher; **b** bank; **c** live; **d** work; **e** work; **f** work

Conversation 2

1 2 children; 9 and 5 years old
2 a two **b** three **c** five years old
3 a :índ-ich awláad?; **b** bass; **c** níHna :índ-na síttah

Language discovery

1 thaláath banáat
2 his and her age

Practice 2

1 a banáat; **b** ikhwáan; **c** akhawáat
2 a awláad, banáat; **b** sanawáat; **c** akhawáat
3 a -ha; **b** -uh; **c** -hum
a my daughter is four years old; **b** my brother is six years old;
c the boys/children are three and eight years old

Reading Arabic

a5; **b**6; **c**1; **d**8; **e**7; **f**4; **g**2; **h**3

Test yourself

1 a housewife (lit. master (f) of the house)
2 a Nizwa, Oman; **b** 20; **c** engineer; **d** three
3 a :úmr-i; **b** ti-shtaghal-íin; **c** :úmr-uh; **d** tí-skun; **e** yi-shtághal

REVIEW 1–3

1 c
2 a5; **b**7; **c**1; **d**3; **e**6; **f**2; **g**4
3 a ínti; **b** ínti; **c** ínta; **d** ínta
4 a3; **b**1; **c**4; **d**5; **e**2
5 a5; **b**4; **c**2; **d**1; **e**3
6 a ingliz-íyyah; **b** gaTar-íyyah; **c** Tabíib-ah; **d** mudárris-ah; **e** amriik-íyyah
7 a I am English; **b** I am Qatari; **c** I am a doctor; **d** I am a teacher;
e I am American

8 a ithnáin	2	٢
b :áshara	10	١٠
c khámsah	5	٥
d thaláathah	3	٣
e sába:ah	7	٧
f wáaHid	1	١
g thamáanyah	8	٨

9 a ána ísm-i...; **b** ána min ...; **c** á-skun fii ...; **d** ná:am/laa; **e** ragam
tilifóon-i ...; **f** a-stághal al-Hiin fii ...; **g** ná:am :índ-i.../laa, ma :índ-i awláad
10 a
11 a the second word; **b** al-baríid

UNIT 4

Hours of the day

2 (Monday), 4 (Wednesday), 5 (Thursday)

Vocabulary builder

p.m. (evening)

New expressions

three; open; open; closed; ashkúr-ich

Conversation 1

1 four hours
2 7.30
3 half an hour
4 if there is one, when it closes in the evening

Language discovery

1 as-sáa:ah sáb:ah
2 húwwa magfúul al-Hiin

Practice 1

1 a 4:15; **b** 4:40; **c** 8:30; **d** 11:05; **e** 2:25
2 a as-sáa:ah khámsah; **b** as-sáa:ah :ásharah wa nuSS; **c** as-sáa:ah thaláathah ílla rúba::; **d** as-sáa:ah wáaHidah wa nuSS wa khams; **e** as-sáa:ah sáb:ah wa thilth; **f** as-sáa:ah ithná:shar ílla :áshar
3 a maftúH; **b** maftúHah; **c** magfúul; **d** maftúH; **e** magfúulah

Listen and understand

1 a 8:00; **b** 9:30; **c** 4:05; **d** 3:45; **e** 7:10; **f** 11.55
3 as-sáa:ah ...

Conversation 2

1 post office
2 closed (all day) on Friday
3 yes
4 all day every day until midnight

Language discovery

1 magfúul yoom al-júma:ah
2 c Saturday evening
3 it closes at 12 o'clock at night

Now your turn!

a al-másbaH yí-ftaH as-sáa:ah kam yoom al-árba:ah aS-Súbah?

b al-máT:am yi-bánnid as-sáa:ah kam yoom as-sabt fi l-lail?

Practice 2

1 a al-bank yí-ftaH as-sáa:ah kam?

yí-ftaH as-sáa:ah thamáanyah aS-SúbaH.

b al-mool yí-ftaH as-sáa:ah kam?

yí-ftaH as-sáa:ah tís:ah aS-SúbaH.

c as-síinima ti-bánnid as-sáa:ah kam?

ti-bánnid as-sáa:ah iHdá:ashr wa nuSS fi l-lail.

d márkaz ash-shúrTah yí-ftaH as-sáa:ah kam?

yí-ftaH as-sáa:ah sáb:ah wa rúba: aS-SúbaH.

e ad-dukkáan yi-bánnid as-sáa:ah kam?

yi-bánnid as-sáa:ah wáaHdah wa nuSS ba:d aDH-DHuhr.

2 a 11:30; **b** 9:10; **c** 7:25; **d** 12:15; **e** 15:00; **f** 23:55

3 7 a.m. to 11 p.m.

Reading Arabic

1 a E; **b** B; **c** M, E; **d** M; **e** M; **f** B; **g** M; **h** E

Test yourself

1 a as-sáa:ah thamáanyah aS-SubaH

b as-sáa:ah thintain wa nuSS ba:d aDH-DHuhr

c as-sáa:ah síttah wa :áshar fi l-lail

d as-sáa:ah árba:ah ba:d aDH-DHuhr

e as-sáa:ah :ásharah ílla rúba: aS-SubaH

f as-sáa:ah khámsah wa rúba: fi l-lail

g as-sáa:ah sáb:ah wa nuSS aS-SubaH

h as-sáa:ah iHdá:ashar wa thilth fi l-lail

2 a yoom ath-thaláathah

b yoom as-sabt

c yoom al-khamíis

d yoom al-júma:ah

e yoom al-ithnáin

f yoom al-áHad

UNIT 5

Shopping

How much is the khanjar (dagger)?

Conversation 1

1 incense burner
2 a F; **b** T; **c** T; **d** F
3 a6; **b**4; **c**1; **d**5; **e**3; **f**2

Language discovery

a ákbar; **b** a-ríid; a-shúuf

Practice 1

1 a4; **b**2; **c**6; **d**1; **e**3; **f**5
2 new incense burner, frankincense, big shirt, old ring
3 a :índ-ak tháani áSghar?
b :índ-ak tháaniyah árkhaS?
c :índ-ak tháani áTwal?
d :índ-ak tháaniyah ágSar?
4 a SIM card; **b** coffee pot; **c** beautiful bracelet; **d** cheap watch;
e bigger shirt; **f** longer necklace

Talking about prices

five; cheaper

Conversation 2

1 5 riyals
2 a tamáam, riyaaláin; **b** fiih :índ-ak tháani árkhaS?; **c** ti-sáwwi takhfíiDH?;
d háadha bi-thaláathah riyáal; **e** kill shay gháali!; **f** shay tháani?
3 a too expensive; **b** still too expensive; **c** everything is expensive; **d** two riyals

Language discovery

1 al-áHmar
2 riyaaláin

Numbers 30 to 1,000,000

a The Arabian Nights (lit. (a) thousand nights and (a) night); **b** Ali Baba and the Forty Thieves

Practice 2

1 a Hámra; **b** burtugáali; **c** ákhDHar; **d** áswad; **e** zárga
2 a6; **b**1; **c**5; **d**3; **e**7; **f**2; **g**4
3 a3; **b**4; **c**5; **d**1; **e**2

Reading Arabic

1 a 5M; **b** 7B; **c** 2E; **d** 8E; **e** 3B; **f** 1M and M; **g** 4M and M; **h** 6B

Test yourself

as-saláamu :aláikum; a-ríid a-shtári silsílah; :índ-ak tháaniyah áTwal?; shúkran. híyya jadíidah?; háadhi bikám?; háadhi gháaliyah; bíshtari

UNIT 6

Food and drink

a mashruubáat **b** sandwíicháat

Vocabulary builder

milk, sugar, juice, with, cola

Conversation 1

1 tea
2 a3; **b**4; **c**1; **d**2
3 aT; **b**F; **c**T; **d**T; **e**F

Language discovery

1 a aish :índ-kum min mashrubáat?; **b** :índ-na gáhwah
2 a ána a-Híbb :aSíir; **b** ána maa a-Híbb shaay; **c** ána a-fáDHDHal gáHwah

Practice 1

1 a6; **b**3; **c**10; **d**2; **e**1; **f**8; **g**9; **h**4; **i**7; **j**5
2 a6; **b**5; **c**2; **d**3; **e**1; **f**4
3 a2; **b**4; **c**1; **d**3

Listen and understand

1c; **2**f; **3**b; **4**a; **5**d; **6**e
2 a i; **b** ii; **c** ii; **d** ii

New expressions

falafel, houmous, cake

Now your turn!

ána jaw:áan! ána áa-khudh bárgar wa chibs, min fáDHlak.

Conversation 2

1 chicken salad with chips, cheese sandwich, burger, bread with houmous
2 a3; **b**5; **c**2; **d**1; **e**4

Language discovery

1 íntu jaw:aan-íin?
2 aish ti-riid-úun?
3 aish ti-ríid?
4 ti-riid-úun khubz?

Practice 2

1 a5; **b**3; **c**6; **d**1; **e**2; **f**4
2 **a** cheese sandwich; **b** burger and fries; **c** falafel and houmous
3 a2; **b**3; **c**1
4 a4; **b**5; **c**2; **d**6; **e**1; **f**3; **g**8; **h**7
5 **a** íntu :aTshaan-íin? **b** aish ti-riid-úun ti-shrib-úun? **c** ti-faDHDHal-úun gáhwah aw shaay? **d** bi-Halíib aw bi-súkkar? **e** ti-riid-úun sandwíich? **f** bi-l-jíbin aw bi-d-dajáaj?

Reading Arabic

1 aM; **b**B; **c**E; **d**M; **e**B; **f**M; **g**M; **h**E
2 a7; **b**8; **c**4; **d**6; **e**1; **f**3; **g**2; **h**5
3 a3 restaurant; **b**1 exit only; **c**2 no photography

Test yourself

a masáa' an-nuur. aish :índ-kum min mashruubáat? **b** aish :índ-kum min :aSíir? **c** ána báa-khudh :aSíir Tuffáh. aish :índ-kum min sandwiicháat? **d** a:Tíini bárgar wa baTáaTa. **e** laa, bidúun SálaTah. **f** shúkran

REVIEW 4–6

1 **a** thaláathah; **b** wa; **c** sáb:ah, nuSS; **d** ílla
2 **a** a.m. **b** p.m. **c** p.m. **d** a.m.
3 fiih másbaH (hína) fi l-fúndug?
4 a6; **b**3; **c**4; **d**7; **e**1; **f**5; **g**2
5 **a** as-síinima tíftaH as-sáa:ah kam?
b al-máT:am yibánnid as-sáa:ah kam?

c al-mool yíftaH as-sáa:ah tís:ah wa nuss.
d al-másbaH yibánnid as-sáa:ah sáb:ah fi l-lail.
6 a ٥٣ (53); **b** ٤٥ (45); **c** ٢٣٠ (230); **d** ٢٩ (29); **e** ٨٧ (87); **f** ٢٠٠٠ (2000)
7 a masculine – húwwa, háadha
b feminine – híyya, háadhi
8 a M – ring; **b** F – necklace, chain; **c** M – incense burner; **d** F – SIM card;
e M – dress; **f** M – shirt
9 a wrong – háadhi zoolíyyah jamíilah.
b correct
c wrong – háadha finjáan rakhíiS.
d wrong – háadhi silsílah Tawíilah.
a This is a beautiful carpet.
b This is a big incense burner.
c This is a cheap coffee cup.
d This is a long necklace.
10 a4 big; **b**3 small; **c**5 cheap; **d**6 expensive; **e**1 short; **f**2 tall; **g**7 beautiful
11
:índ-ak tháani ákbar
:índ-ak tháani áSghar
:índ-ak tháani árkhaS
:índ-ak tháani ághla
:índ-ak tháani ágSar
:índ-ak tháani áTwal
:índ-ak tháani ájmal
12

a :índ[-i]		*I have*
b :índ[-uh]		*he has*
c :índ[-na]		*we have*
d :índ[-hum]		*they have*
e :índ[-ich]		*you (f) have*

13 a4; **b**1; **c**2; **d**3
14 a-ríid/áa-khudh/a:Tíini:
a :aSíir laimóon bi súkkar
b sandwíich wa kóola
c gáhwah wa kaik

15 a al-fúndug – others are days
b thaláathah – others are multiples of ten
c zoolíyyah – others are colours
d :aSíir laimóon – others are foods
16 c (speed limit is 50)
17 a D3; **b** G4; **c** H7; **d** A8; **e** F2; **f** E1; **g** B6; **h** C5

UNIT 7

Getting around the city

fish market

Vocabulary builder

mosque, supermarket, fish market
left, right

Conversation 1

1 go straight on
2 a4; **b**3; **c**1; **d**2
3 a laa, maa á:raf; **b** ruuH síidah; **c** ba:dáin liff yamíin;
d al-bank ba:íid :an hína?
4 a F; **b** T; **c** T; **d** F – five minutes away

Language discovery

1 a fiih baríid garíib min hína? **b** laa, maa fiih.
2 ruuH síidah

Practice 1

1 fúndug, márkaz ash-shúrTah, máT:am, Saydalíyyah, mustáshfa
2 a3; **b**1; **c**2
3 a4; **b**1; **c**2; **d**3
4 a liff; **b** ruuH; **c** liff
5 a fiih baríid garíib min hína?
b fiih mustáshfa garíibah min hína?
c fiih márkaz ash-shúrTah garíib min hína?
d fiih mátHaf garíib min hína?

e fiih fúndug garíib min hína?
f fiih Saydalíiyyah garíibah min hína?
g fiih mádrasah garíibah min hína?
h fiih suug as-sámak garíib min hína?
6 a al-baríid ba:íid :an hína?
b al-mustáshfa ba:íidah :an hína?
c al-márkaz ash-shúrTah ba:íid :an hína?
d al-mátHaf ba:íid :an hína?
e al-fúndug ba:íid :an hína?
f aS-Saydalíiyyah ba:íidah :an hína?
g al-mádrasah ba:íidah :an hína?

Listen and understand

1 a hospital (fiih); **b** hotel (maa fiih); **c** market (maa fiih); **d** shop (fiih);
e museum (maa fiih); **f** cinema (fiih); **g** pharmacy (fiih);
2 a C2; **b** D4; **c** A3; **d** B1

New expressions

hotel, hotel, right, left

Conversation 2

1 fúndug ash-shams (lit. Sun Hotel)
2 Don't speed up!
3 straight, roundabout, right, second, right, 50, restaurant

Language discovery

a khudh tháani sháari: :ála l-yamíin; **b** jamb máT:am al-khalíij

Practice 2

1 a3; **b**7; **c**1; **d**5; **e**8; **f**4; **g**2; **h**6
2 a khudh áwwal sháari: :ála l-yamíin; **b** khudh tháalith sháari: :ála l-yisáar;
c khudh ráabi: sháari: :ála l-yamíin wa ba:dáin liff yisáar; **d** khudh tháani
sháari: :ála l-yamíin wa ba:dáin ruuH síidah; **e** :ind ad-duwwáar liff yisáar
3 a khúdhi áwwal sháari: :ála l-yamíin; **b** khúdhi tháalith sháari: :ála
l-yisáar; **c** khúdhi ráabi: sháari: :ála l-yamíin wa ba:dáin líffi yisáar;
d khúdhi tháani sháari: :ála l-yamíin wa ba:dáin rúuHi síidah;
e :ind ad-duwwáar líffi yisáar

4 a pharmacy; **b** go straight, at the roundabout turn right; **c** on the left;
d next to the restaurant
5 a al-wálad fi l-máT:am; **b** as-síinima ba:d márkaz ash-shúrTah; **c** al-baríid
gábil as-subermáarkit; **d** aS-Saydalíyyah jamb al-mátHaf; **e** as-sayyáarah
taHt al-jisr; **f** al-fúndug ba:d al-másjid

Reading Arabic

1 a street; **b** lúghah; **c** on; **d** after; **e** :aSíir; **f** expensive; **g** :umáan;
h Baghdad
2 :árabi (Arabic)
4 a2; **b**1

Test yourself

1 samáHt, wain, rúuH, yamíin, tháani, :ála, ba:d, as-suug, fiih, maa
2 a fiih máT:am garíib min hína; **b** al-báHar min wain; **c** kaif arúuH
as-síinima min hína
3 a ruuH síidah; **b** líffi yisáar wa ba:dáin rúuHi síidah; **c** ruuH síidah wa
ba:dáin khudh tháani sháari: :ála l-yamíin; **d** laa, maa fiih bank garíib min
hína; **e** suug as-sámak jamb al-míina

UNIT 8

Getting out and about

a mitru; **b** mawgif al-baaS

Vocabulary builder

taxi, metro

New expressions

bus, two, plane

Conversation 1

1 return
2 a false – 125 riyals; **b** false – 8 a.m.; **c** true
3 a fiih baaS yiruuH mubaasharatan; **b** at-tadhkarah bi-kam? **c** al-baaS
yiTla: as-saa:ah kam?; **d** mata yoosal ad-dooHah?; **e** a:Tiini tadhkarat
dhiháab w iyáab Hagg baakir.

Language discovery

a a:Tiini tadhkarat dhiháab w iyáab
b fiih baaS yiruuH ad-dubáy min faDHlak?

Practice 1

1 a3; **b**5; **c**4; **d**1; **e**2

2 a yiruuH; **b** mubaasharatan; **c** bi-kam; **d** iyáab; **e** yiTla:; **f** mata;
g as-saa:ah; **h** Hagg

3 a True; **b** False (leave in Sohar at 09:00); **c** False (not direct);
d True

4 a 4; **b** 5; **c**2; **d**3; **e**1

Listen and understand

1 a return; **b** one-way; **c** return; **d** one-way

2 a fiih baaS yiruuH abu DHabi; **b** fiih baaS yiruuH masqat; **c** fiih baaS
yiruuH ar-riyaaDH; **d** fiih baaS yiruuH Salalah.

3 SabaaH al-khair.
fiih giTaar yiruuH ar-riyaaDH baakir ba:d aDH-DHuhr?
yiTla: as-saa:ah kam?
yooSal as-saa:ah kam fi r-riyaaDH?
tádhkarat dhiháab w iyáab bikam?

New expressions

four-wheel drive/4x4; day; days

Conversation 2

1 4W drive

2 a new, very nice/beautiful; **b** does it have A/C; **c** two days; **d** 300 Dh;
e yes; **f** Saturday 4 p.m.

3 a hiyya sayyaarah waajid jamiilah; **b** dagiigah min faDHlak; **c** yoom
as-sabt, nafs al-wagt; **d** as-saa:ah kam laazim arajji:ha

Language discovery

a :ishriin laitir mumtaaz; **b** mumkin tichayyik al-aayil?

Practice 2

a4; **b**3; **c**2; **d**5; **e**1

Reading Arabic

a4; **b**3; **c**2; **d**1

Test yourself

a fiih baaS yiruuH abu DHabi?
b mata yooSal?
c tadhkarat dhiháab (bass) bi-kam?
d :Tiini tadhkarat dhiháab w iyáab.
e ariid asta'jir sayyaarah min faDHlak.
f kam al-iijaar li-usbuu: waaHid?
g mumkin adfa: bi l-kart?

UNIT 9

Leisure

Do you like soccer/football?

Vocabulary builder

music, squash, cinema, television

New expressions

soccer/football

Conversation 1

1 soccer/football
2 a2; **b**3; **c**1
3 a4; **b**5; **c**1; **d**2; **e**3
4 a False – he plays with friends; **b** False – he doesn't like football; **c** True;
d False – Thursday

Language discovery

a marrtain fi l-usbuu::; **b** aHyaanan; **c** aruuH al:ab; **d** nijlis fi l-bait; **e** bashuufak

Now your turn!

a aHyaanan; **b** kull or kill; **c** marrah; **d** daayman; **e** ba:d

Practice 1

1 a5; **b**6; **c**9; **d**2; **e**3; **f**7; **g**8; **h**1; **i**4
2 a3; **b**5; **c**1; **d**2; **e**6; **f**4
3 a3; **b**4; **c**5; **d**2; **e**1
4 a4 bitruuH; **b**3 biyruuH; **c**2 bashuuf; **d**1 binsawwi

Listen and understand

1 a tennis – every day after work
b cinema – twice a month
c beach (with friends) – sometimes

d mall – always on Thursdays
e market – never
2 sometimes (aHyaanan), with friends (Sadiigaat), shopping
(aruuH as-suug), cinema (as-siinima), sport (ar-riyaaDHah), swimming
(as-sibaaHah), I don't like (maa aHibb), in shaa 'Allaah
3 a5; **b**4; **c**1; **d**2; **e**3

New expressions

do you think, tomorrow

Conversation 2

1 to visit Salma and Shamsa
2 a go to the mall; **b** going the day after tomorrow (with sister); **c** visit
Salma and Shamsah; **d** 10 o'clock

Language discovery

a wain tiriidiin tiruuHiin; **b** tiriidiin tiruuHiin al-mool?; **c** mumkin nruuH
nzuur salma wa shamsa

Practice 2

1 a aruuH ashuuf fiilm fi s-siinima.
b aruuH amshi :ala l-baHar.
c aruuH azuur ahl-ii fii sidaab.
d aruuH al:ab goolf ma: Sadiig-i.
e aruuH agra' fi l-Hadiigah.
f aruuH at:allam al-lughah al-yabaaniyyah.
2 There are various possibilities – exercise 1 supplies suggested answers.

Reading Arabic

1 a laam and waaw; **b** miim; **c** miim, waaw, laam; **d** miim (appears twice);
e laam; **f** waaw, laam, meem, haa'
2 a as-suuq; **b** máktab; **c** dubáy mool; **d** mumtaaz; **e** Haliib; **f** doorat
al-miyah

Test yourself

1 a Hibb/maa aHibb a al-ghooS; **b** ar-riyaaDah; **c** as-sibaaHah;
d at-takhayyam
2 a ana bal:ab kurah; **b** niHna binal:ab skwaash; **c** inta bitshuuf
at-tilifizyoon; **d** huwwa biyruuH al-mool
3 The answers for this depend on your own preferences.

4 laa, ana faaDHi.
mumkin nal:ab kurah :ala l-baHar.
as-saa:ah khamsah
ashuuf-ak baakir in shaa' Allaah
ma:a as-salaamah

UNIT 10

Holiday time

a min máayo li sabtámbar; **b** ijáazat aS-Saif; **c** jábal

Vocabulary builder

April, August, December

New expressions

year, first, we, I, plane, car, I, we

Conversation 1

1 The Emirates and Oman
2 a5; **b**1; **c**4; **d**2; **e**3
3 a T; **b** F; **c** F – visited museums in Sharjah; **d** T
4 a iii; **b** i; **c** iv

Language discovery

a ruHt; **b** shufna; **c** sawwaina; **d** zurt

Now your turn!

a la:bt, sáafart, rája:t, takállamt, ishtághalt, sábaHt, shárabt
b la:bna, sáafarna, rája:na, takállamna, ishtághalna, sábaHna, shárabna

Practice 1

1 a2; **b**3; **c**1
2 a3; **b**4; **c**5; **d**1; **e**6; **f**2
3 ams ... **a** ana ruHt as-siinima; **b** huwwa sharab gahwah; **c** niHna zurna al-matHaf; **d** inti ruHti al-mool; **e** huwwa ishtaghal fi l-máktab; **f** humma raaHu suug adh-dhahab.
4 Yesterday ... **a** I went to the cinema; **b** he drank coffee; **c** we visited the museum; **d** you (f) went to the shopping mall; **e** he worked in the office; **f** they went to the gold market.
5 a F; **b** F; **c** T; **d** NT; **e** F; **f** T; **g** F
6 a with her sister **b** her sister bought new clothes; **e** her brother visited the Sheikh Zayed Grand Mosque; **g** her friend Charlotte visited the water park

8

	morning	afternoon
a	went to shopping mall	visited parents
b	watched TV in the house	worked in the office
c	visited sister Fatima	went to cinema with husband
d	played football with friends	made trip to beach

Conversation 2

1 a2; **b**5; **c**4; **d**1; **e**3

2 a

3 c

4 b

5 a kaan al-jaww Haarr; **b** kaan fiih bard w maTar; **c** kunt fii brizban yoomain bass

Now your turn!

1 a kunt fi d- dooHah al-usbuu: al-maaDHi; **b** kaan al maT:am magfuul yoom al-juma:ah; **c** kaan al-fiilm waajid zain; **d** kaan :induh bait kabiir fii landan; **e** kaan fiih waajid naas fi s-suug ams

Practice 2

1 a3; **b**6; **c**5; **d**1; **e**2; **f**4

2 a kaan al-jaww baarid; **b** kaan fiih maTar; **c** kaan fiih Harr; **d** kaan al-jaww muu zain; **e** kaan fiih thalj; **f** kaan al-jaww baarid

3 a3; **b**4; **c**1; **d**5; **e**6; **f**2

Reading Arabic

1

a Something to eat – as-samak (fish) السمك

b Something to drink – al-qahwah (coffee) القهوة

c A way to travel – bi s-sayyaraah (by car) بالسيارة

d A day of the week – sabt (Saturday) سبت

2 a fish; **b** coffee; **c** car; **d** Saturday

3 a ana uHibbu s-samak

b ashrabu l-qahwah kull yoom

c saafartu ila dubáy bi s-sayyaarah

d al-maT:am maftuuH kull yoom sabt

4 a I like fish; **b** I drink coffee every day; **c** I travelled to Dubai by car; **d** The restaurant is open every Saturday

Test yourself

1 a shuft at-tilifizyoon; **b** sharabt (finjaan) gahwah; **c** la:bt tanis; **d** ruHt as-siinima

REVIEW UNITS 7–10

1 a6; **b**5; **c**2; **d**1; **e**4; **f**3

2 a cinema

b football

c swimming and diving

d squash

e meeting up or going to the market with friends

f music, staying at home, watching TV

3 a law samaHt, al-baHar min wain?

b law samaHti, as-suug min wain?

c law samaHti, aS-SaydalÍiyah min wain?

d law samaHt, al-maTaar min wain?

e law samaHt, al-bank min wain?

f law samaHti, as- as-súubermarkit min wain?

4 fiih; maa fiih

5 a4; **b**1; **c**6; **d**5; **e**3; **f**2

6 i, d, a, g, e, h, c, f, b

7 a kurah; **b** jalsah; **c** sibaaHah; **d** musiiga; **e** siinima; **f** aruuH al-mool

8 a al-jaww zain al-yoom

b kaif al-jaww fi l-baHrain?

c kaan al-jaww baarid

d kaan fiih maTar aS-SubaH

e darajat il-Haraarah sittah wa thalaathiin

9 a falaafil (the others are weather)

b bi-sukkar (the others are transport)

c azrag (the others are verbs in the *I*-form)

d fi s-suug (the others are time adverbs/phrases)

e kam (the others are prepositions)

f sawwaag at-taaksi (the others are places in town)

10 a b-(or bi-); **b** kaan (m), kaanat (f); **c** -i

11 a 6; **b** 5; **c** 4; **d** 3; **e** 1; **f** 2

12 mars, maayo, yuulyo, aghusTos, nufambar, disambar

13 a P; **b** F; **c** F; **d** P; **e** f; **f** P

14 train

15 a medicine (Saydaliyyah is *a pharmacy*)
16 b
17 c 25 to 50 per cent
18 a shurTah
19 a 18 dirham; **b** 17 dirham; **c** medium
20 a F – opens at 10 a.m.; **b** T; **c** F – closes at midnight on Saturday

Core vocabulary

:áa'ilah (pl. -áat)	*family*
:áadi	*regular (petrol), normal*
:ála	*on*
:ámal	*work (noun)*
:arábi/-íyyah	*Arab/Arabic (m./f.)*
:aSíir	*juice*
:aTsháan	*thirsty*
:ind	*at, by, with* (used for *to have*)
:umáan	*Oman*
:úmr	*life, age*
ab (*also* wáalid)	*father*
ábadan	*never*
ábyaDH (f. báiDHa)	*white*
áHmar (f. Hámra)	*red*
áHsan	*better*
aHyáanan	*sometimes*
áiDHan (*also* ba:d)	*also*
aish?	*what?*
ákbar	*bigger*
akh (pl. ikhwáan)	*brother*
akhbáar	*news*
ákhDHar (f. kháDHra)	*green*
ákil	*food*
ákthar	*more*
al-Hiin	*now*
al-khalíij (al-arábi)	*(the) Gulf*
al-yoom	*today*
almáaniya	*Germany*
amáam	*in front of*
amríika	*America*
ams	*yesterday*
ána	*I*
áSfar (f. Sáfra)	*yellow*
ash-sharq/ash-sharg al-áwsaT	*Middle East, the*
ásra:	*faster, fastest*
áswad (f. sóoda)	*black*
aw	*or*
áwwal	*first*
áwwalan	*firstly, first of all*
ayy	*any, which?*
ázraq/ázrag (f. zárqa/zárga)	*blue*

ba:d	after, also, still
ba:d aDH-Dhuhr	afternoon (lit. after the noon)
ba:dáin	then, afterwards, later
báachir/báakir/búkrah	tomorrow
báarid	cold (adj)
baaS (pl. -áat)	bus
báHar	sea/beach
baHráin (al-)	Bahrain
báiDHah (pl. baiDH)	egg
bait (pl. buyúut)	house/home
bank (pl. bunúuk)	bank
bantalóon	trousers
bard	cold (noun)
bárgar, bárghar	burger
baríid	post office
bass	only, enough
baTáaTa	fries
bi DH-DHábt	exactly
bi-	with, by, in
bi-dúun	without
bi-kháir	well
biláad (f.) (pl. buldáan)	country
bint (pl. banáat)	girl, daughter
bi-l-Halíib (also bi-Halíib)	with milk
briTáaniya	Britain
burj (pl. abráaj)	tower
burtuqáali/burtuqáali/-yah	orange (colour) (m./f.)
burtuqáal/burtugáal	orange (fruit)
dáayman	always
dagíigah (pl. dagáayig)	minute
dajáaj	chicken (collective noun)
dárajah (pl. -áat)	degree
dawwáar	roundabout
dháhab	gold
diháab	single/one-way (ticket)
DHúh(u)r	noon
dóorat al-miyáah	bathrooms, restrooms
dukkáan	shop (small)
fáaDHi/-yah (m./f.)	free, also empty
faránsa	France
fii	in
fiih	there is, there are
fiilm (pl. afláam)	movie
fíkrah	idea
finjáan (pl. fanajíin)	coffee cup
fooq/foog	up, above
fúndug/fúnduq (pl. fanáadig)	hotel

gháali/-yah	*expensive* (m./f.)
ghaim	*clouds*
gharb	*west*
ghooS	*diving*
háadha/f. háadhi/pl. haadhóol	*this, these*
Haal	*condition*
Haarr	*hot*
Hagg	*for*
Hálaq/Hálag	*earrings*
Halíib	*milk*
Hílu/Hílwah	*sweet*, also *great, cool* (m./f.)
Haráarah	*heat*
Harr	*heat*
háwa	*wind*
hína/híni	*here*
híyya	*she*
húmma	*they*
húwwa	*he*
ílla	*except*
imaaráat	*Emirates*
imaaráat (al-)	*(the) Emirates*
ingiltárra	*England*
inglíizi/-íiyyah	*English* (m./f.)
ínta	*you* (m, sing.)
ínti	*you* (f, sing.)
íntu	*you* (pl.)
isbáanya	*Spain*
iskutlánda	*Scotland*
iTáaliya	*Italy*
jábal (pl. jibáal)	*mountain*
jadíid/-ah	*new* (m./f.)
jálsah	*hanging out, picnic, barbecue*
jamb	*next to*
jamíil/-ah	*beautiful* (m./f.)
jaw:áan/-ah	*hungry* (m./f.)
jazíilan	*very much* (after **shukran** thanks)
jib(i)n	*cheese*
jíddan (*also* wáajid)	*very*
jinsíiyyah (pl. -áat)	*nationality*
kabíir/-ah	*big* (m./f.)
kaif?	*how?*
kaik	*cake*
kam?	*how much/many?*
kathíir/-ah	*a lot, many/much* (m./f.)
khoor	*creek*
kídha	*that sort of thing, like this/that*

kill shay, *also* kull shay	everything
kill, kull	every
kitáab (pl. kútub)	book
kúrah	soccer/football
kuwáit (al-)	Kuwait
láakin	but
láazim	necessary, must
lail (*general*); lailah (*single night*)	night
laimóon	lemon
laish?	why?
li-	to
lúghah (pl. -áat)	language
má:a	with, together with
maa	not (before verbs)
máaDHi (-iyah)	last (e.g. week, year) (m./f.)
maay	water
madíinah (pl. múdun)	city
madrásah (pl. madáaris)	school
maftúuH/-ah	open (m./f.)
maqfúul/magfúul/-ah	closed (m./f.)
makáan (pl. -áat)	place
máktab (pl. makáatib)	office
márkaz ash-shúrTah	police station
márkaz tijáari	shopping centre
márkib (pl. maráakib)	boat
márrah (pl. marráat)	time, occasion (pl. sometimes)
márrah tháaniyaah	again (lit. a second time)
márrah/marr(a)táin	once/twice
mása	evening
másbaH	swimming pool
mashghúul/-ah	busy (m./f.)
mashrúub (pl. mashruubáat)	drink
másjid	mosque
máT:am (pl. maTáa:im)	restaurant
máta?	when?
maTáar	airport
máTar	rain
mátHaf (pl. matáaHif)	museum
mawjúud/-ah	present, here (m./f.)
máwqif/máwgif (pl. mawáaqif)	parking
min	from
mool	shopping mall
mubáasharatan	directly
mudárris/-ah	teacher (m./f.)
múmkin	possible
mumtáaz	excellent, super, premium (gasoline)

mushkílah (pl. masháakil)	*problem*
musíiqa/musíiga	*music*
mustáshfa (f.)	*hospital*
muu	*not* (before nouns and adjectives)
na:náa:	*mint*
níHna	*we*
nuSS	*half*
qábil/gábil	*before*
qadíim/gadíim/-ah	*old* (m./f.)
qáHwah/gáhwah	*coffee*
qaríib/garíib/-ah	*near* (m./f.)
qaSíir/gaSíir/-ah	*short* (m./f.)
qáTar/gáTar	*Qatar*
qiTáar/giTáar (pl. -áat)	*train*
ra'y	*opinion*
rajjáal (pl. rajajíil)	*man*
rakhíiS/-ah	*cheap* (m./f.)
ráqam/rágam	*number*
ráqam/rágam tilifóon	*phone number*
ríHlah (pl. -áat)	*journey, trip*
riyáaDHah	*sport*
rúba:	*quarter*
sáa:ah (pl. -áat)	*hour, clock, watch*
Sadíiq/Sadíig (pl. aSdiqáa')	*friend* (m.)
Sadíiqah/Sadíigah (pl. -áat)	*friend* (f.)
Saghíir/-ah	*small* (m./f.)
Saif	*summer*
SálaTah	*salad*
sámak	*fish* (collective noun)
sánah (pl. sanawáat)	*year*
sarii:/-ah	*fast* (m./f.)
Sayd as-sámak	*fishing*
Saydalíiyyah	*pharmacy*
sayyáarah (pl. -áat)	*car*
sháari:	*street*
shaay	*tea*
sháhar (pl. shuhúur)	*month*
shamáal	*north*
shams	*sun*
shárikah (pl. -áat)	*company*
sharq/sharg	*east*
shay (pl. ashyáa)	*thing*
shibs	*potato crisps*
shíishah/maHáTTat banzíin	*petrol station*
shíta	*winter*
shúghal	*work*

shwáyya	little (amount)
sí:ir	price
síidah	straight on
síinima (f.)	cinema
SabaH	morning
súkkar	sugar
súubermarkit	supermarket
suuq/suug (pl. aswáag)	market, souk
Táalib/-ah	student (m./f.)
Tabíib/-ah	doctor (m./f.)
tádhkarah (pl. tadháakir)	ticket
taH(i)t	down, under
taqríiban/tagríiban	approximately
tasáwwaq	shopping
Tawíil/-ah	long (m./f.)
Tayyáarah (pl. -áat)	plane
tháani/-yah	another, second (one) (m./f.)
thalj	snow, ice
tilifizyóon	television
tilifóon	mobile/phone
ukht (pl. akhawáat)	sister
umm (*also* wáalidah)	mother
usbúu:	week
ustráaliya	Australia
wa	and
wáajid (*also* jíddan)	very, much, many
wáalid (*also* ab)	father
wáalidah (*also* umm)	mother
waalidáin	parents
wain?	where?
wálad (awláad)	boy/son (pl. also means children)
waqt/wagt al-faráagh	time/free time
wára	behind
wásaT	centre, medium, middle
yamíin	right
yisaar (*also* shimáal)	left
yoom	day
zooj	husband
zóojah	wife

Useful phrases

:áfwan	*you're welcome*
:an ídhnik	*excuse me*
áasif, áasfah	*sorry*
áhlan wa sáhlan	*hello, welcome*
as-saláamu :alaikum	*hello*
ashkúr-ak/-ich	*thank you* (formal)
áywa, also ná:am	*yes*
bikám?	*how much?* (price)
fii amáan Allaah	*goodbye* (lit. *May God keep you safe*)
Hayyáa-k Allaah	*thank you, goodbye* (lit. *God give you life*)
in shaa' Allaah	*God willing*
khalíini afákkir	*let me think*
laa	*no*
law samáHt/-i	*please, excuse me* (m/f)
ma:a s-saláamah	*goodbye*
maa fiih	*there isn't/aren't*
maa sháa' Allaah	*My goodness! Wow!*
min fáDHlak/-ich	*please* (m/f)
muu mushkílah!	*no problem!*
ná:am, (*also* áywa)	*yes*
nzain (*also* zain)	*good, fine*
shúkran	*thank you*
shwáyya	*a little*
shwáyya shwáyya	*slowly*
Tab:an	*of course*
tamáam	*good, fine*
Táyyib	*OK, good, fine*
tfáDHDHal/-i	*here you are* (m/f) (when giving something to someone)
wa :aláikum as-saláam	*hello* (in reply to **as-saláamu :alaikum**)
ya jamáa:ah	*Hey, everyone!*
yá:ani	*well, ... um, kind of*
zain (*also* nzain)	*good, well, fine*

List of verbs

Here is a list of verbs which appear in *Beginners' Arabic*. In each case, the *he* form of the past tense is given first, followed by the *he* form of the present tense. Remember to note where the stress lies.

:áraf/yí:raf	*to know*
á:Ta/yá:Ti	*to give*
ákhadh/yáakhúdh	*to take*
aráad/yaríid	*to want, wish*
ashtára/yishtári	*to buy*
bánnad/yibánnid	*it closes* (m/f)
cháyyik, yicháyyik	*to check*
dáfa:/yídfa:	*to pay*
fátaH/yíftaH	*it opens* (m/f)
ishtághal/yishtághal	*to work*
ishtára/yishtári	*to buy*
istá'jar/yistá'jir	*to rent, hire*
jálas/yíjlis	*to stay, sit, remain*
kaan/káanat	*was* (m/f)
lá:ab/yíl:ab	*to play*
laff, yilíff	*to turn* (direction)
laff/yilíff	*to turn to* (direction)
naam/yináam	*to sleep*
qára/yíqra gára/yígra	*to read*
raaH/yirúH	*to go*
rajja:/yirájji:	*to return something*
sáafar/yisáafir	*to travel*
sákan/yískun	*to live*
sáwwa/yisáwwi	*to do, make*
shaaf/yishúuf	*to see, look at*
ta:állam/yit:állam	*to learn*
Tála:/yíTla:	*to leave, go out*
wáSal/yóoSal	*to arrive*
zaar/yizúur	*to visit*

Acknowledgements

We would like to thank the following people for their kindness to us during the writing of this book: the Battashi family, in particular Saif and Fatimah al-Battashi; Kirsty Christer and Azza al-Harthi for their generous assistance; Joanna Groves, Dawn and Simon Thompson, Malinka van der Gaauw, Andy Figgins, Sawad Adogla, Fionnuala Quirke, Deborah Hennigan and all friends and family for their practical and moral support. Special thanks are due to Eid Yusef and Ahmed Chbib for their invaluable contributions, support, and for always being on hand.

Many thanks, also, to all our editors at Teach Yourself. We are grateful for all their help, patience and encouragement.

Last but by no means least, we dedicate this book to the memory of Jack Smart. It is because of his life-long commitment to the Arabic language, which has inspired so many, and his passion and enthusiasm for the countries and the people of the Arab world, that we have been able to write this book.

Frances Altorfer

Mairi Smart

Photo credits

All photographs were supplied by the authors and are the copyright of Frances Altorfer and Mairi Smart unless specified otherwise.

Artworks 1 and 9 on p. 119 and 1 a on p. 141 were illustrated by Nadene Naude (Beehive Illustration).

Can-do statements

UNIT	CEFR level	ACTFL level	CAN-DO STATEMENTS
UNIT 1	A1	Novice High	I can establish basic social contact by saying where I am from and by using simple everyday polite forms of greetings, farewells and introductions.
UNIT 2	A1	Novice High	I can ask for and provide personal information and can use numbers effectively.
UNIT 3	A1	Novice High	I can ask and answer questions about myself and other people, where I live and what I do for a living. I can describe my family.
UNIT 4	A1	Novice High	I can indicate time by such phrases as 'three o'clock'. I can communicate in simple and routine tasks requiring a simple and direct exchange of information.
UNIT 5	A2	Intermediate Low	I can ask about things and make simple transactions in shops.
UNIT 6	A2	Intermediate Low	I can interact with reasonable ease provided the other person talks slowly and clearly and is prepared to help. I can say what I like and dislike.

UNIT	CEFR level	ACTFL level	CAN-DO STATEMENTS
UNIT 7	A2	Intermediate Low	I can deal with common aspects of everyday living such as travel. I can ask for and understand simple directions relating to how to get from X to Y, by foot or public transport.
UNIT 8	A2	Intermediate Low	I can get simple information about travel, use public transport such as buses, trains and taxis, and buy tickets.
UNIT 9	A2	Intermediate Low	I can make arrangements to meet, decide where to go and what to do next. I can understand everyday signs and notices in public places.
UNIT 10	A2	Intermediate Low	I can communicate in simple and routine tasks requiring a simple and direct exchange of information on familiar activities. I can describe past activities and personal experiences.